To my dear friend Phil,

  In memory of the past,

    Author Mary.

June 1973

Also by May Eustace

CATS IN CLOVER
TOP CATS
CAT UP

Photo: Dr Brian Eustace

Richmond Show. 1901. Judges: Miss Frances Simpson and Mr
C. A. House, editor of *Fur and Feather*. (Photograph from *The
Book of the Cat* by permission of Cassell & Co.

Fifty Years
of Pedigree Cats

MAY EUSTACE
&
ELIZABETH TOWE

PELHAM BOOKS

First published in Great Britain by
PELHAM BOOKS LTD
26 Bloomsbury Street
*London. W.C.*1
1967

Set and printed in Great Britain by Tonbridge Printers
Ltd, Peach Hall Works, Tonbridge, Kent, in Bell twelve on
thirteen point, and bound by James Burn at Esher, Surrey

ACKNOWLEDGEMENTS

Grateful acknowledgement is made to:

Miss Mary G. Duff, BSc. (Glasgow) & MRCVS for her articles on Modern Veterinary Treatment and Silver Tabby Long-Hairs.

Professor R. Turner for Notes on Line Breeding and Understanding Genes.

Mr V. Watson for notes on eye colour in Burmese, reprinted from *Fur and Feather*.

The National Geographic Society, Washington DC, for the extract from PANTHER ON THE HEARTH by Frederick B. Eddy, National Geographic, 1938.

Hutchinson Publishing Co. for extract on THE TEMPLE CAT by M. Oldfield from Howey's THE MYSTERIES OF RELIGION AND MAGIC.

Methuen & Co. for permission to quote lines from Sir Compton MacKenzie's INTRODUCTION to Phyl Wade's THE SIAMESE CAT.

Sir Isaac Pitman & Sons for quotes from Frances Simpson's CATS FOR PLEASURE AND PROFIT.

The Governing Council of the Cat Fancy, Australia and Victoria, (Inc) extracts from *The Cat World*.

Mrs Joan Thompson for quotations from *Our Cats*.

Mrs E. Fisher for her notes on the Birman Cat.

Miss Turner for her notes on Foreign Whites.

Mr R. Steele's letter concerning Wild Cats.

The Northern Press Ltd. for short quote in *Shields Gazette*.

The Editor of *Fur and Feather* for permission for short quotes.

Mrs Grace Pond of the National Cat Club for short extract on Persian Cats.

Miss Lynn Hamilton for poems quoted from her book, SOPHISTI-CATS, published by Chapman and Grimes, Boston, 1949.

The Governing Council of the Cat Fancy for permission to reprint their Standard of Points and other data.

Miss K. Macpherson for the loan of otherwise unobtainable books.

The authors and publisher wish also to thank all those who kindly allowed their photographs to be included in this book.

CONTENTS

CONTENTS

1 Origin and Early History of the Cat

'If any of my readers hunger and thirst for information concerning the descent of the cat through marsupial ancestors and mesozoic mammals to the generalized placental or monodelphous carnivara of today let them consult . . .'

Extract: *Concerning The Origin Of The Cat*
Helen M. Winslow, 1900

Very little is known about the origin of the cat. Archeologists and zoologists who have made a careful study of fossil remains, stone carvings, ancient paintings, and old manuscripts believe that the pre-historic cat was descended from a small, vicious, carnivore, with short legs and a long body, which inhabited this earth millions of years ago. This creature was described as a Miacus. Others connected with this carnivore were of the weasel family, which at some time or other took the shapes of stoats, and civets, and ferrets. When one or other of these creatures finally became a cat, is one of the mysteries of animal creation.

Many nineteenth century writers made exhaustive studies of the origin of the cat and contributed largely to the spreading of knowledge and the invention of folk-lore, which was very palatable to cat lovers of that age. The best known of these writers were: Ross, who had published in England in 1868 *The Book of the Cats*, St George Mivert's, *The Cat*, again published in England in 1881, Mrs Cashel Hoey's translation from the French, of

Campfleury's, *The Cat Past and Present*, in 1884, and Harrison Weir's, *Our Cats and All About Them*, published in 1889. *Moncrif's Cats*, written in the form of letters appeared in 1727, and was a model for many later cat books.

These writers, and many more, strove earnestly to establish proof of the origin of the cat. This was inconclusive, for even St George Mivert, whose book was probably the most exhaustive and complete of any, was forced to admit that he found little proof. 'On the whole, it seems probable that the mammalia, and therefore the cat, descends from some highly developed, somewhat reptile-like batrachian of which no trace has ever been found'.

In the same way knowledge of the origin of the domestic cat is acknowledged to be obscure, if non-existent. One of the most important and well-informed of contemporary writers, Brian Vesey-FitzGerald, wrote: 'I do not know the origin of the domestic cat. Nobody does. The plain and incontrovertible fact is that we have no definite knowledge at all of the domestic cat.'

Nevertheless, we twentieth century cat lovers cling to our traditions. Simple faith dies hard. It is pleasant to contemplate the cat in Ancient Egypt placed on a very high pedestal, assuming the grandeur of a Goddess, holding the sistrim in her hands which was the symbol of the harmony of creation. In the Egyptian Gallery at the British Museum, where hieroglyphics can be interpreted, the high place of the cat is defined. It is almost certain that for nearly 2,000 years BC cats were domesticated in Egypt, where they were worshipped as Gods. Their mummified remains were found interred with their masters.

Campfleury, writing about the cats in Ancient Egypt, says he can find no proof of how the cat was introduced into the country of the Pharaohs, but Egyptologists have not found any representation of the cat upon buildings 'contemporaneous with the pyramids.' He writes, 'The cat appears to have been acclimatised at the same time with the horse, at the beginning of the new empire (about 1668 BC). The most ancient version of the Ritual of the Dead of which we have any knowledge, goes no further back. At that epoch we find the cat represented in mural paintings, sitting under the armchair of the mistress of the house; a position also occupied by monkeys and dogs. The rarity and the utility of the cat probably led to its admission to the ranks of sacred animals, with a view to its systematic propagation. Its utility is attested by paintings representing sporting scenes in the marshy valleys of the Nile, where cats plunge into the water to retrieve and carry the game.'

It is thought that cats were introduced into Greece and Rome by Phoenician traders but there was not the same interest as in Egypt. The Romans were most likely to have brought cats to Britain, and all cat historians welcome further authenticity of cats in the Code of Howell the Good, a Welsh king, which was enacted some time about AD. 920 This was known as the Vendotian Code:

(1) The worth of a kitten from the night it is kittened until it shall open its eyes, is one penny.
(2) And from that time until it shall kill mice, two pence.
(3) And after it shall kill mice, four legal pence; and so it shall remain.

There also was written the Dimentian Code, and the Gwentian Code, all giving importance to the cat. Another Welsh law says, 'Three animals reach their worth in a year; a sheep, a cat and a cur' and, in order that there should be no confusion in the mind as to what a cat looked like, it was roughly sketched on the manuscript.

The Celtic people, especially the Irish, gave great prominence to cats in legend and song, and Lady Gregory's, Book of Saints And Wonders, brings into the picture with great interest, a mysterious cat. The land known as 'The Isle Of Saints And Scholars', could have added to its title, 'The Isle Of Saints And Scholars And Cats'. There are many beautiful and remarkable tales of the cat, and, in our time when the revival of the Irish language became so important to Irish people, many old translations brought up to date for general interest, gave preference to the cat above any known domestic animal.

In Europe, there were many vicissitudes in store for the little cat. He was not to tread unmolested through the aeons of time. Because of the aureola of mystery that surrounded him he was never ignored. He was loved much, and hated much. Hate showed itself in the practice of atrocious cruelties. He was regularly burned at the stake, sometimes in company with equally hated witch women. The burning of cats became a ritual. At one time, 'It was considered an encouragement to good behaviour to throw a few cats into the fire at the Festival Of St John,' said a French writer, M. du Merie, and he was also quoted as saying that the Prior of a Monastery could produce receipts for, 'having supplied for three years all the cats required for the fire on St John's Day'.

But it is difficult to separate what is legendary from reality or to be shocked beyond measure at the cruelties practised on defenceless animals by human beings, for the sufferings of animals were on a par with the sufferings that human beings inflicted on each other. One has only to glance at the Newgate Calendar and read of the penalties exacted for thieving; even small children were hung for petty offences.

From the seventeenth century onwards, important names began to be associated with cats. Painters, writers, politicians, statesmen, poets, churchmen and men of many letters gave patronage to the cat. The cat's virtues were extolled, but most of all was he admired for his independence.

Campfleury, in his stylish nineteenth century language says, 'Man has desired the society of the cat. The cat has not sought the society of man. Let the animal roam in peace about woods or gardens; it will not ask to come in to dessert, and to stretch itself upon the drawing-room carpet. The cat will suffice to its own needs; it will find its food, and sleep in a tree. One week of freedom will restore its natural independence to the cat.'

In English literature there are many references to the cat. Boswell, writing about Dr Johnson and his cat, Hodge, gives a most touching description of the love between this human and his cat. These lines have become a classic and one can almost hear the purr of Hodge, when after being at first humiliated he was then highly praised: 'I recollect him one day scrambling up Dr Johnson's breast, apparently with much satisfaction, while my friend, smiling and half whistling, rubbed down his back, and pulled him by the tail; and when I observed he was a fine cat, saying, "Why, yes sir, but I have had cats whom I like better than this,"; and then, as if perceiving Hodge to be out of countenance, adding, "but he is a fine cat, a very fine cat indeed".'

And another of the incidents written about the same Hodge, was when Boswell heard Dr Johnson remonstrate with his wife for speaking sharply to him in the servant's hearing in case they might have been encouraged to do likewise.

Sir Walter Scott, in his old age, became a great cat lover and Victor Hugo, the poet, though very much attached to cats, surprisingly admitted that they could be lazy. When asked why his cat was called 'Chanoine' he smilingly retorted that it was because he was slothful and idle, and thereupon stroked the limp and lazy form of his much beloved Chanoine.

Moncrif, the writer of, *Lettres sur les chats*, was the cat lover par excellence of early eighteenth century France. He was not a slave of one cat but of many as revealed in his writings. His unique 'gravely frivolous book' as he himself called it, was said to have been inspired by an evening amongst an intelligensia of cat-haters, when the prejudices against cats were publicly aired causing Moncrif such great irritation that he wrote to his friend, *Lettres sur les chats*, expatiating on the virtues of cats. He did not then think of publication.

Amongst prominent cat-loving churchmen, Cardinal Richelieu was the most famous. He was slightly different to many because it was in kittens he had most interest. Their antics amused and distracted him. His gruff manners and habitually bad humour, were often alleviated by the soothing presence of kittens, which he liked to have near to use as an antidote against depression. The ill-fated Cardinal Wolsey, when summoned to the presence of his Master for what he knew would be a final dismissal, touched his little cat whose favourite resting place was amongst his state papers, saying, 'All my friends have deserted me, save you, Matou.'

Mark Twain's reference to cats is very often quoted and it is so intimate and homely that the repetition of it has found favour amongst many cat lovers today:

'A house without a cat, and a well-fed, well-petted, and properly revered cat, may be a perfect house, perhaps, but how can it prove its title'.

Because of the poise and dignity of a cat, he has very often been included in famous paintings. One, which has given substance to many beliefs about the existence of cats in the far back ages is Durer's Adam & Eve in which a cat creeps into the Garden of Eden. Rembrandt selected a cat as a suitable animal to appear in his picture of the Virgin and Child. Renoir also gave a cat to the girl in his wonderful painting of Girl With A Cat. In the National Gallery alone, if cats could be enticed from their canvases to join in a cat cavalcade, what a spectacle of delight it would be for twentieth century catophiles!

Then, as the new age on invention illuminated the lives of humans, the little cat began to reap the benefits. A new awareness of things, and people, and creatures was created. Situations taken for granted hitherto, now became matters of great moment. Life on earth was changing, and soon the spirit of competition would set up new values and new ways of thinking. Man was the first being to put himself on show. Since the days of the stone age personal beauty had always been a cult. The spirit of competition and exhibition was ingrained in the human race. It was only by comparison with others that his own merit was achieved. So too, with the lesser race, the subordinates of man, the animals. Through centuries they have stood against each other; horse racing, dog racing, bull fighting, cock fights, parades, exhibitions and shows; in one form or another this competition between animals of a sort has gone on. Again, it is only by competition, one with the other, that the merit of each is declared.

But these early shows were haphazard and lacked control, resulting in fraction and bitterness, and by the middle nineties the need for organization began to show itself. Dog shows got on the way a very short time before cat shows and it will be interesting to Northern readers to note that the first recorded dog show was held in Newcastle upon Tyne in 1859, nearly twenty years before the establishment of the Kennel Club. This club was founded in 1873, and because of the tremendous interest in dogs it was an immediate success. Soon the administration of canine affairs was adopted and standards for the showing of dogs were published. The first dog show run under Kennel Club rules was held at the Royal Aquarium in 1886. This site is now known as The Central Hall, Westminster, the venue for so many cat shows. Associated with this first show was the magic name of Charles Cruft, the great pioneer of dog show managing. Then commenced the annual shows which were soon to be the greatest dog shows in the world. Few people in the world today have not heard of Cruft's Show at Olympia.

Though in the Cat Fancy we had no Charles Cruft to give immortality by title to our greatest and most important shows, we had, in the shape of Harrison Weir,

mentioned in the opening paragraphs, a great Victorian
gentleman, endowed with the pioneering spirit of Cruft,
who set things rolling for cat lovers. He held the first
organized cat show at the Crystal Palace in 1871. Though
the National Cat Club was not formed until a few years
later the first Harrison Weir Show kindled the flames of
what was soon to be known as the British Cat Fancy.
Luckily for us, twentieth century cat fanciers, Harrison
Weir gave something to cat-loving posterity, when, in
1899, he sat down and wrote and illustrated his now rare
and valuable book, *Our Cats and All About Them*. Describing this first cat show, to which he had induced his anti-cat
friend to come, he says, 'Inside the Crystal Palace stood
my friend and I. Instead of the noise and struggles to
escape, there lay the cats in their different pens, reclining
on crimson cushions, making no sound save now and then
a homely purring, as from time to time they lapped the
nice new milk provided for them. Yes, there they were,
big cats, very big cats, middling-sized cats, and small cats,
cats of all colours and markings, and beautiful pure white
Persian cats; and as we passed down the front of the cages
I saw my friend become interested; presently he said,
"What a beauty this is! and here's another!" "And no
doubt," said I, "many of the cats you have seen before
would be quite as beautiful if they were as well cared for
or at least cared for at all; generally they are driven about
and ill-fed, and often ill-used, simply for the reason that
they are cats, and for no other." '.

And so the Cat Fancy was born!

This First Cat Show was a triumph for Harrison's
Weir's capacity for organization. Gone from the show
bench were the frivolities and indecisions of previous
attempts. Now a system of judging was agreed and the
judges had before them a standard of points and cats were
entered in classes suitable to their breeds. A book of rules
was given to each exhibitor, with instructions about show
preparation and other necessary information for all new-

comers. The first judges to be nominated were, of course, Harrison Weir himself, his brother John Jenner Weir, and the Rev. J. Macdona. All men. This one-sided all male cast did not find favour with many women, who were shortly to gate-crash in amongst the doyens of the new Cat Fancy. American writer Miss Helen M. Winslow, from whom I stole the pompous introductory passage to this chapter, said of men judges, 'American cat shows have at least three judges, one of them at least should be a woman. A cat should be handled gently and kept as calm as possible during the judging. Women are naturally more gentle in their methods, and more tender-hearted. When *my* pets are entered for competition, may some wise, kind women have the judging of them!'

The standard of points set out by Harrison Weir was comprehensive and intelligible. He brought to the Cat Fancy a seriousness compatible with knowledge and deep understanding which had previously manifested itself in his many other activities. He was a man of many callings, being journalist, commercial artist and voluminous writer of works on animals, and his thoroughness in finding factual evidence and checking references was clearly illustrated in a book, *Our Poultry and All About Them* which had occupied him for over twenty years. This book contained 600,000 words, 37 coloured pictures and 350 black and white drawings. We cat fanciers of the twentieth century are very lucky indeed that Harrison Weir decided to share with cats his profligacy of words.

The most favoured of all Harrison Weir's breeds were the magnificent White Persians with eyes, 'Large, full, round or almond-shaped, lustrous and of a beautiful azure blue', and Colour of Coat, 'White, with a tender, very slightly yellow tint; cushions of feet and tip of nose pink'. For all the Long Hairs there were the same requirements as to Fur and Quality of Fur; 'Very long everywhere, mostly along the back, sides, legs, and feet, making tufts between the toes, and points at the apex of the ears. The quality of the fur should be fine, silky, and very soft in the Persian, with a slightly woolly texture in the Angora, and still more in the Russian'. Eye colour varied for each different breed, setting a pattern to match coat colour; 'For Black, orange. For Blue, orange-yellow. For Grey, deep yellow. For Red, gold, tinged with green, and should be very large, round, or almond-shaped, full and very bright'.

Altogether, with Long-Hairs alone, in addition to White there were Black, Blue, Grey, Red, or any Self Colour, and of the Tabby variety he had named Brown, Blue, Silver, Light Grey, and White Tabby. Altogether this was quite a formidable classification for the First Cat Show set to Rules, known in the world.

And then came the Short-Hairs, which were even more numerous still. In Short-Hairs too, Harrison Weir had his preferences, and from his writings I would say he was most intrigued by The Tortoiseshell which he studied very carefully, and divided the breed into two kinds, as we do today – Tortoiseshell and Tortoiseshell and White. Most points were allotted for colour, which was 'A mixture of three colours – black, red and yellow, each to be distinct and clear of the other with sharp edges, not one colour running into the other, but in small irregular patches, of great brilliancy of tint, the red and yellow to preponderate over the black. If the colours are deep and rich, and the variegation harmonious, the effect is very fine. In this breed white is a disqualification.' In the Tortoiseshell and White, the colour is the same, with the addition of White Markings. 'The fore-legs, breast, throat, lips and a circle round them, with a blaze up the forehead, white; lower half of the hind-legs, nose and cushions of the feet, white.'

The other Short-Hairs listed were White, Self-colour, Black, Grey or Red, and in Tabbies, Brown and ordinary striped Tabby, Chocolate, Chestnut, Red or yellow striped, and Blue, Silver, Light Grey, and White striped Tabby. Then came Spotted Tabbies of any colour, and the very ordinary Black and White, Grey-White, and Red and White, and to carry it even further, Harrison Weir reversed order and gave breed numbers to White and Black, White and Grey, and White and Any Other Colour.

In quiet relief there were shown the interesting foreign breeds, and the Abyssinian, reputed to have come straight from Africa in 1868, was even in those days, demoted for showing White, but most interesting was the description of Carriage And Appearance which said, 'Graceful, lithe, elegant, alert and quick in all its movements, head carried up, tail trailing, in walk, undulating.' Altogether, a code of definition, whose classic contours revealed his noble heritage. The Manx, or Short-Tailed Cat got short shift, as the tail question was not definitely clarified and must have mystified the judges. 'To have no tail whatever, not even a stump, but some true bred have a very short, thin twisted tail that cannot be straightened; this is allowable and is true breed; but thick stumps, knobs, or short thick tail disqualify.'

The Royal Cat of Siam had its 100 points allocated very differently to ours of today, as type did not seem to matter as much as colour and markings. But in one reckoning there was no difference for the marks for tail were the same. The 5 points given for this appendage may not be the anachronism it is today, for the breed was not yet developed. How absurd would a judge look who had put up for championship honours a Siamese cat with a tail that was stumpy, short, twisted or even non-existent, and yet he was top having scored the full 95 marks for all his other good qualities?

Harrison Weir's detailed study and final summing up of the 'Points of Excellence' was most impressive, but one cannot help but feel a little sympathy for the solid figures of Victorian manhood, who were, in turn, scholar, writer and churchman, but had now deviated from their own fields of learning, and had come thither to the Crystal

Palace, to sort out the wheat from the chaff, at this first feline exhibition. But this sorting out must have been done to the satisfaction of the promoter, for Harrison Weir carried to his dying day, on his watch chain, the silver bell that his Blue Tabby 'The Old Lady', won on the day she made her debut at the Crystal Palace in 1871. And for himself and his endeavours and his 'labour of love of the feline race, and acting without fee, gratuity or reward' he received from the Crystal Palace Company a presentation of a silver tankard.

The important show brought together important people. Cats were the topic of the day. Around each pen little groups of folk congregated and introductions were made. 'They were of all sorts and creeds, but they had an affinity with each other closer than marital bonds. Whatever other days may bring, today they were of one fold.'

At this first cat show new friendships commenced, and, to cement these friendships the idea of a cat club was mooted. Very soon indeed the National Cat Club was founded, and Harrison Weir was elected to be the first President. In 1898, another club was founded and this was known as The Cat Club, and into its ranks came the fairest in the land. The Presidents were: His Grace the Duke of Bedford, and Lord Marcus Beresford. The Vice-Presidents, about ten in number, were so gilt-edged and imposing that it would appear that they walked straight from the House of Lords.

The commencement of record keeping got on the way with a stud book, and the cats whose names were inscribed were no less regal than their patrons. Blue Boy The Great of Islington and his spouse, Mimidatzi of Bridgeyate, were amongst early contenders for initiation to the new ranks of Fancy Cats; also the famous U.S.A. blue male, Beadle, who had commenced his show career in England under the humble title of Bumble Bee, got his name in too. It would appear that this youthful feline had no compunction about changing names, never having heard that over here in England this can only be done by Deed Poll!

So, in the dying years of the last century, cat clubs saw their beginnings. The well-established Cat Club whispered into the receptive ears of this new race of cat fanciers its seal and motto:

'Beauty lives by kindness'.

2 *The First Cat Fanciers*

A cablegram to the *New York Evening Sun* arrived from London on the 4th January, 1906, and read: 'Harrison Weir, artist, author and journalist, died here today at the age of 82. He was on the original staff of the *Illustrated London News* and the last survivor of it. He was connected with the London *Field*, *Graphic*, *Black and White*, *Poultry* and other periodicals. For more than fifty years Mr Weir was judge at all the principal poultry and pigeon shows and was also designer of race cups for Goodwood and Ascot, and for the Jewellers, Garrard & Co. In his later years he became absorbed with cats and was the originator of the cat show which is now held annually at the Crystal Palace'.

Harrison Weir lived long enough to see that the pedigree cat was accepted; also that organized cat shows were welcomed and the Cat Fancy firmly established. His carefully set out Standard of Points became the yardstick for cat breeders of all ages.

But Harrison Weir was not only an organizer and expert planner, he was also the most distinguished cat lover of the new age. He studied cats in all their moods, and left behind for us his observations. Being a very careful judge (and he set his own standards) the exhibit presented to him was literally 'turned upside down and inside out'. His comments on the behaviour of the cat during this 'agony' are amusing. Though his first and last loves were the Persians he recorded in his judge's notes that they were not as sweet-tempered as the Short-Hairs. 'As far as my experience extends, and I have had numerous opportunities of noticing, I find this variety (Long-Hairs) less reliable as regards temper than the short-haired cat. In some cases I have found them to be of almost a savage disposition, biting and snapping more like a dog than a cat, and using their claws less for protective purposes. Nor have I found them so "cossety" in their ways as those of the Short-Hairs though I have found exceptions in both. I may here remark that during the time I have acted as judge at cat shows, which is now over eighteen years, it has been seldom there has been any displays of temper in the Short-Hair breed in comparison to the Long; though some of the former, in some odd instances, have not comported themselves with that sweetness and amiability of a disposition that is their usual characteristic. My attendant has been frequently wounded in our endeavour to examine the fur, dentition, etc. of the Angora, Persian or Russian; and only once been severely bitten by a Short-Hair.

'Hitherto I have been so fortunate as to escape all injury but this I attribute to my close observation of the countenance and expression of the cat about to be handled, so as to be perfectly on my guard, and to the knowledge of how to put my hands out of harm's way'.

Harrison Weir on Persians

But Harrison Weir did not content himself with being a judge with a cool exterior; he also studied his little friends from the vantage point of an observer only.

'I noticed one cat at the last Crystal Palace show, a white cat (note that all his favoured ones are white–Author) it looked up, it looked down, then to the right and then a little to the left, paused, seemed lost in thought, when, not seeing anyone about, it crept over to the door, and with its paws tried to pull back the bolt or catch. On getting sight of me, it retired to a corner of the cage, shut its eyes and pretended to sleep. I stood further away, and soon saw the paws coming through the bars again. This cat had noticed how the cage door was fastened, and so knew how to open it.'

Harrison Weir

It is certain that judges, exhibitors and spectators alike, reading these observations today would like nothing better than to witness this game of 'Peep-O' between the greatest fancier of the day and the little white cat.

Though Harrison Weir was of a serious and reserved nature, most of the cat stories that he retained were humorous. In one of his memos he quoted a letter that he had received from a person, telling all about his prize cat which he had acquired through the good offices of the President of the Cat Club, a close friend of his. After a full page of eulogies the new owner dealt on the practical side of owning a pedigree cat.

My dear friend,

. . . And now to your suggestion about the hole in the door. Nessa did not take to this at all. She much preferred to struggle with the latch and make her way out in an honourable way as befitting an important cat. After a lot of practice and many bumps on to the tiles, she now has perfected the art of opening the kitchen door, and this is the way she likes best to make her escape, but no matter how I try to coax her, tempting her with rare delicacies, I have never succeeded in teaching her how to close the door. I wonder if I ever shall.

S. S. Potter

I take the liberty of replying to Reverend S. S. Potter, 'No. You never will.'

And talking about holes in the doors to allow cats to come and go as they please, Sir Isaac Newton thought out something cleverer; when his cat wanted to take her kitten in the garden, the great cat lover had two holes made, one for the mother cat and one for the kitten.

And so the Cat Fancy grew and grew.

The late nineties and the early years of the new century were days of elegance for the pedigree cat. He had been adopted by the right kind of people, and was welcomed into the homes of the most important people in the land. Show cats were on the highest plane of all, for by being put on exhibition they and their forbears and their important breeders had to be named. This gave a great cachet to the pedigree cat.

Royal patronage influenced considerably the general opinion in England for the breeding and exhibiting of pedigree cats was a hobby of the rich and influential. Queen Victoria and the Prince of Wales were known to have attended cat shows, and it is recorded that, a trophy, in the form of a signed and framed photograph of the Prince of Wales was won by a beautiful Blue Persian, named Patrick Blue. The wording of the award said:

'For Best Blue Long Hair in the show; to be awarded irrespective of sex or nationality'.

This famous Blue also won the Beresford Challenge Cup at the first Championship Show of the National Cat Club.

Lady Marcus Beresford was the most well-known and influential person in the new Cat Fancy. She pioneered the commercial breeding of pedigree cats, having set herself up in business, with large catteries, stud cats and queens and kittens of every variety, but, once again, it was to Blue Persians she was most attracted.

She was certainly the first woman in the world to be bitten by the Cat Show bug. The visiting of cat shows to her became an all-absorbing hobby and it was stated that she sometimes took as many as thirty cats to a show, arriving with a retinue of followers which with cats in the seat of honour resembled very much a Royal Ascot procession of today. Her vast array of felines stormed show venues from the Crystal Palace in London to the Railway Grounds in Harrogate. These pioneer show managers had the right ideas about going places, for they brought their shows into the country to entice fanciers who might have been isolated.

Lady Marcus's catteries were world famous. At one

time she had over 150 cats in residence, and 'residence' meant a high style of living. To keep these cats well-fed and housed, she employed full-time help, which included two kennel maids and a youth who performed the rougher tasks. Lady Marcus herself described the management: 'There is a small kitchen for cooking the meals for the cats, and this is fitted with every requisite. On the walls are racks to hold the white enamelled bowls and plates used for the food. There is a medicine chest, which contains everything that is needful for prompt and efficient treatment of the sick. On the wall are a list of the names and a full description of all the inmates of the Cattery, and a set of Rules to be observed by both the cats and their attendants. These Rules are not ignored, and it is a tribute to the intelligence of the cat to see how carefully pussy can become amenable to discipline, if one is given to understand of what that discipline consists.

Regarding the diet of the inmates of the cattery, they were served up most appetizing bowls of fish and rice, and sometimes mince-meat was mixed with the rice. Also she kept a goat on the premises to supply milk for delicate kittens.

The Hon. Mrs McLaren Morrison was another gracious lady whose devotion to cats was nearly as great as was Lady Marcus Beresford's, and was also associated with the Cat Club as vice-president. She was described as being 'one of the most attractive and fascinating women of the day – one who adds to personal beauty all the charm of mental culture and much travel'. In her many excursions her cats always went with her, sometimes to her town residence in Queen Ann's Mansions, and even as far away as to Calcutta. Her stately home at Kepwick Park in Yorkshire had listed as cattery occupants every known type of cat but her breeding stock were mostly Blue Persians, though she also possessed Blacks, Silvers and Reds, English type Silver Tabbies, Russians, also Chinese cats with golden eyes and long, pointed chins. Best known of her Blue Persians was Champion Monarch, who won many prizes.

Many of the most beautiful cats bred in those early days were exported abroad, and laid the foundation stone of new Cat Fancies in far-away lands. However, those anxious to keep tags on important cats found it difficult because of the custom amongst new owners of changing names. There were no known prefixes as we have today, and cats could appear at one show under one name and appear again re-christened and re-furbished.

A great number of these fancy English cats made their way to the U.S.A., where they found in Mrs Clinton Loche a Lady Marcus Beresford and a Mrs McLaren Morrison rolled into one. She too believed in safety in numbers for at a show of the Beresford Cat Club held in Chicago, she exhibited fifteen cats of the one colour. The American Cat Fancy was helped on considerably by her enthusiasm and interest. Again, though, many of her cats were English bred, they lost their identity, for the reason I have stated.

It cannot be disputed but that Persian cats adorned the first scenes to be set in England for pedigree cats. Though very rare and valuable, they were known in these isles for centuries. It was recorded that they were first imported from Italy as long ago as 1551 by one Pietro L'Aval. Whether these very early specimens bore any resemblance to the first registered Long-Hairs is very difficult to estimate. It is not disputed, however, that their careful development was done in England, for on the continent, for many years they were described as, 'Made in England', and, 'English Masterpieces of selective breeding'. The Persian cat was, and is recognized, as the most impressive of all cats, for in addition to his magnificent long silky coat, he has a distinctive round head, crowned by tiny ears, and he has the most beautiful eyes of any animal in the world.

Harrison Weir's first Standard of Points bulked all

colours and varieties together, with no special emphasis on the very important Blues; this was rather surprising as even then Blues were the outstanding Long-Hairs. Certainly by the turn of the century their popularity had gained momentum and they were the cats of the new era.

In spite of all the efforts made to assess values and give 'points' to the Short-Hair cats, they never really, in those days, became fancy cats. This was because they were so ordinary and so numerous that no one could be convinced of their value. It would be difficult to fall head over heels in love and give new value to a creature whose breeding habits necessitated the annihilation of many of its off-spring. A great cat lover, writing an appreciation of her friend, lately deceased, in *The Club Woman* in 1891, says of her, 'She was the gentlest, kindest and most noble friend I have ever had. She would not hurt a fly. When the destruction of Blackie's, her beloved cat's kittens became necessary, she always drowned them in hot water, for she said, "it would not be such a shock to the poor little things as plunging them into cold water".' So, it would seem, 'kind' hearts had sometimes to be unkind. It is therefore not difficult to understand that people did not quickly readjust themselves to new values for the common, ordinary household cat.

Frances Simpson, a judge and important fancier, writing a little later in *Cats And All About Them*, expresses the opinion of many known breeders of the day. 'The commonest of all cats are Short-Haired Tabbies and Whites and Blacks. We see these specimens on many doorsteps. The markings are sometimes quite grotesque in their distribution. It seems almost a pity to so far encourage these cats as to give classes for them at our shows.' In spite of this castigation of the commoners there were some important Short Hairs in England. All breeders of Short-Hair Silver Tabbies have heard of Champion Timmy, who was said by his owner to be worth £1,000.

The British Blue and the Russian were confused. There did not seem to be evidence of the foreign type in the latter. Alone, being unmistakably foreign, were the rare Abyssinians. The origin of this breed has always caused controversy amongst breeders. It is reputed that Abyssinians came straight from Africa about the year 1868; they were not unknown to Harrison when he set out his standards. It is certain that this cat most nearly resembles the first cat of the Pharaoh's, and the distinctive contours, if superimposed on old etchings, would leave little doubt in the minds of the most cynical that the Abyssinian has naught but a noble heritage.

But it was to the common cat that late nineteenth century writers gave immortality. Agnes Repplier, the American writer of famous animal stories, wrote of her beloved commoner, Agrippina; 'Agrippina's beautifully ringed tail flapping across my copy distracts my attention and imperils the neatness of my penmanship. Even when she is disposed to be affable, turns the light of her countenance upon me, watches with attentive curiosity every stroke I make, and softly, with curved paws, pats my pen as it travels over the paper, even in those halcyon moments, though my self-love is flattered by her condension, I am aware that I should work better and more rapidly if I denied myself this charming companionship. But, in truth, it is impossible for a lover of cats to banish these alert, gentle, and discriminating little friends, who give us just enough of their regard and complaisance to make us hunger for more . . . How many times have I rested tired eyes on her graceful little body, curled up in a ball and wrapped round with her tail like a parcel; or stretched out luxuriously on my bed, one paw coyly covering her face, the other curved gently inwards as though clasping an invisible treasure. Asleep or awake, in rest or in motion, Agrippina is always beautiful; and it is better to be beautiful than to fetch and carry from the rising to the setting of the sun'. And then the writer, in the most poetic and appealing language, describes how Agrippina settles herself to sleep.

'Slowly the eyes close, gently the little body is relaxed. Oh, you who strive to relieve your overwrought nerves and cultivate power through repose, watch the exquisite languor of a drowsy cat and despair of ever initiating such perfect and restful grace. There is a gradual yielding of every muscle to the soft persuasiveness of slumber; the flexible frame is curved into tender lines, the head nestles lower, the paws are tucked out of sight; no convulsive throb or start betrays a rebellious alertness; only a faint quiver of unconscious satisfaction, a faint heaving of the tawny sides, a faint gleam of the half-shut yellow eyes, and Agrippina is asleep. I look at her for one wistful moment and then turn resolutely to my work. It were ignoble to wish myself in her place; and yet how charming to be able to settle down to a nap "sans peur et sans reproche" at ten o'clock in the morning.'

And this beautiful prose was written in 1892 and has lost nothing in the telling seventy-three years later.

3 *The Good Old Days*

Not everyone wants to be educated; the vast majority of folk prefer to stagnate, having no urge to advance mentally. When, as a result of much study and long investigations, pedigree cats were first established, many cat lovers were unwilling to refurbish their ideas and educate themselves in the new trends that had overtaken the ordinary domestic cat. That there was such a thing as right eye colour, proper texture of coat, shapely limbs, exquisite tails did not matter; neither did they concern themselves with the new breed names like Silver Tabbies and Maltese cats. Only two differences would they admit to; Long-Hair and Short-Hair. Even the most sceptical admitted that these kinds of cats could be separated.

Most of these nineteenth century cat lovers had long memories, and recalled the good old days with nostalgia. Variety was then the spice of life. Any member of the cat family, large or small, fierce or domesticated, would appear on exhibition. The unusual got the greatest welcome. Freaks with bizarre markings or odd eyes would attract. Tail-less and very long-tailed cats were alike in being interesting. Hairless cats and those with over-abundant flowing coats, stood side by side before the judges, but cats of huge dimensions were given the greatest ovation of all. There is, on record from the first show in New York, a cat owned by the American writer Mrs Frances Hodgson Burnett which weighed twenty-two pounds, was three feet long, with a girth of 24 inches.

Another enormous cat, exhibited by a New York artist,

Mr Frederick Danton, was a Blue Persian known as Musjat. His weight was in the twenty-one pound region, and besides strength and brawn he had also beauty. He had been imported from Algiers in 1894, and was valued at several hundred dollars. A great show career was abruptly ended for him when he was, with many other treasures, stolen from the owner's house. Though some of the valuables were recovered, Musjat, the magnificent, was never heard of again.

In England too, cats of enormous sizes surprised many a judge. Frances Simpson, associated with the early days of the Cat Fancy, both as judge and breeder, says in her book:

'In former days there used to be classes at our shows in which cats were judged according to their weight, and no matter what points the cat possessed or did not possess, the heavier took the prize. The most weighty cat I ever handled turned the scale at 20 lbs. I do not think, however, that our pets should be fattened up like prize pigs for shows, and, therefore, these weight classes have been wisely done away with'.

The large cat could always gather round him many admirers of less inquiring kind, but the fierce, half-domesticated cat drew the attention of many important fellow travellers. These were zoologists and naturalists, and their interest lent great kudos to the old-time shows. They liked to investigate any rare specimens of the cat family, especially those not far removed from the wild state. Many of these semi-wild creatures appeared in England and Scotland during the early part of the last century.

From Scotland, about the year 1830, we read of a tale from the affairs of one Dr Jock McFadden, who was believed to have been a lecturer in Zoology, and whose interest in the cat family inspired him to attempt the breeding of any interesting variety. Though there are no records, and it is not known how the doctor got possession of an animal which was believed to have been a mixture of ocelot and wild cat, it was certain that he tried to show it; somehow or other the animal was bludgeoned into setting off for the exhibition.

The arrival at the show hall of this strange carnivore caused great excitement and uproar, for on its journey it had collected many followers. The procession hither had not been a silent one. As soon as 'Ossie' found himself caged and strapped to a low-back car, he reverted to the jungle state and screamed forth his hate and bitterness against the human race. The furious cat call brought out the folks in their hundreds, and though this display of cat was never intended to be a trailer for a cat show it certainly aroused the mob and by the time the procession had arrived at the show venue, even the police had tagged on, and but for their intervention, 'Ossie' might have gobbled up a spectator or two. However, the removal from the cage proved to be too difficult, and though the doctor tried all the blandishments he knew of he could not make 'Ossie' see reason. There was nothing to do but turn the cart wheel in the other direction and only when the cat sensed that home was in sight did he desist from his vociferousness. This incident took place, of course, before the days of chloroform by mask or sedation by injection; had he lived today the learned doctor would no doubt have silenced him by a rear-end anaesthetic.

But Ossie was not alone in his opposition to being put on show; there is a record of another undomesticated animal, a Wild Cat of Britain, who refused to co-operate. This cat was captured alive by the Duke of Sutherland and did, in fact, arrive at the first Crystal Palace Cat Show in 1871. But this powerful beast fought the show manager with such fierceness that he could not be penned. He was described as a most magnificent animal with great fury in his breast and who kept his ears flattened to his skull in a defiant manner.

B

His visit to the show is recorded in the following manner by Harrison Weir:

'Mr Wilson, the manager of the show, though an excellent naturalist, tried to get it out of the thick-barred, heavy-made travelling case in which it arrived, into one of the ordinary wire show cages, thinking it would appear to better advantage; but in this endeavour he was unsuccessful, the animal resisting all attempts to expel it from the one to the other, making such frantic and determined opposition that the idea had to be abandoned. This was most fortunate, for the wire cages then in use, were afterwards found unequal to confining even the ordinary domestic cat which, in more than one instance, forced the bars apart sufficiently to allow escape. As it was, the wild cat maintained its position, sullenly retiring to one corner of the box, where it scowled, growled, and fought in a most fearful and courageous manner during the time of its exhibition, never once relaxing its savage watchfulness or attempts to injure even those who fed it. I never saw anything more unremittingly ferocious, nor apparently more untamable'.

But more Wild Cats made their way to the Crystal Palace, and in the following year the Earl of Hopetown actually succeeded in penning a Wild Cat of Britain. During the days of the exhibition vast crowds gathered round this pen and great interest was aroused in this breed. Show managers and zoologists advertised wherever they could their desire to locate these cats, but the response was so small that even then they decided that the Wild Cat of Britain was nearly extinct.

About 1873, a Mrs Senger presented another Wild Cat, but this was a hybrid and had inherited a little domestication from its mother, the cat of the family fireside. Many of the hybrids exhibited were of the spotted tabby variety, and were outstanding. Their markings were distinctive and their type magnificent.

Today the Wild Cat of Britain has practically disappeared, but very odd ones are found occasionally in Scotland. These are rarely captured alive, but abandoned kittens have been brought back to try to domesticate, but with very few exceptions, they have proved to be untamable.

A short while ago the *Sunday Express* related a story from the life of a gamekeeper, Mr Ron Steele, who shot a Wild Cat on the estate of his employer, Sir William Keith Murray, in Perthshire, Scotland. Two of the kittens were taken home and given to a domestic cat to rear, which was done successfully, but the kittens grew fiercer, flattening their ears and spitting at any stranger.

Curious about the ultimate fate of these kittens an enquiry to Mr Steele brought the following reply:

> Brae Cottage,
> Ochtentyre,
> Crieff,
> 1.8.65.

Dear Mrs Eustace,

Thanks for your letter asking about Wild Cats. The two which I reared here are now in the Edinburgh Zoo and doing very well. I had them here for about three months, but they were quite untamable. The bigger they grew, the wilder they got.

Wild cats are roamers. They do not stay in one place for very long. They are all the time on the move, even when they have young kittens. If one happens to come upon them suddenly they will immediately make for cover among rocks, or into any hole if easily located. At other times they will lie below a stone and let you pass within feet of them.

Once the male has mated he has no interest in the female, leaving her to bring up her kittens alone. The usual size of a litter is four, and they appear to be very sturdy and leave their mothers at a very early age.

I have often found a large hare at a cat's den. It had

been dragged so far that it had no hair on one side of it. A fully grown cat will only attack if cornered. If attacked by a terrier, he will fight to the kill, if there is no escape possible.

Wild Cats do not like foxes, and I have found that when we have foxes about the cats are scarce. They are swift runners and will outpace a dog. They kill a lot of grouse, but rabbits and hares seem to be their main food.

I have never seen a tame Wild Cat, not certainly after it was fully grown.

I hope I have given you a little help. I have a lot more to say but find it easier to talk than to put it on paper.

Yours sincerely,
Ron Steele.

Recently, Mrs Marie Smith from Balquhidder, showed me a pelt from a Wild Cat her husband had shot in wooded country in Lochearnhead. What a pity he did not bring him back alive, for I am sure, wild though he was, he could not resist Marie's, 'Cead Mile Failte!' (A hundred thousand welcomes!)

It is certain that the most exciting of those 'good old days' cats were those who were lured into the company of humans, with murder in their hearts. Several of these anti-social beings made their way to the London shows and they nearly always hit the headlines. In the U.S.A. too the high-spirited felines got the publicity they courted. In 1889, at a show in New York, there appeared a cat of Wild Cat ancestry but now in the fascinating guise of a magnificent white Persian. This was a unique cat and was valued at 500 dollars. He had been captured in a wild state in the Persian interior, and, for over a year he had been kept in a cage, resisting all attempts at domestication. But he finally abandoned his distrust of humans and actually became the pet of the family. Everything was going well until he was inveigled into making a public appearance at the show. As soon as he discovered that he had been betrayed he sulked and hissed during the two days of his exhibition. As a wild animal he was to the manner born, and drew crowds, but few admired his beauty.

Cats with a 'past' or cats with a record for fidelity, great intelligence, bravery, homing instinct, or any other virtues, were always given a welcome in a show pen. These kind of cats were news.

Keeping a diary is always a fascinating hobby, and no race of folk are so prone to indulge in this hobby as cat lovers. To diary-keeper, Miss Helen Hill Shaw, we owe the following account of a very early show at which her cat came into the limelight.

'Today, June 16th, 1877 has been one of the happiest days of my life. When the store-keeper, from whom I bought Jimmy's rations, told me about the Cat Show I immediately went in search of the promoters. Yes, I was informed, I could make an entry for 6d and I was given a form to fill in. The principal questions to be answered were:

State the breed of cat: Short-Hair: Brown Tabby
State the age of cat   3 years
State the value of cat

To the latter question I added the words £100, not, of course, intended to be taken seriously. To me he was very valuable and to my way of thinking he was the finest cat in Scotland. But, of course, he had no intrinsic value.

Imagine my surprise when I arrived at the Railway Hall and, on a placard at the entrance the following words were written in big print:

COME IN AND SEE THE £100 CAT: Admission 3d
A long queue were waiting for admission, and as I pushed my way in I heard a big navvy say, "I hope the cat will be worth looking at. I was to have gone to the pub with Jim Murray tonight, but, anyway, here I am, and here's me 3d."

And when I saw Jimmy he was surrounded by an admiring crowd and on his neck was a big rosette, marked

First Prize. On top of his pen was the award; a basket of green vegetables!

Yes, whatever other days may bring, June 16th, 1877 will always stand out in my memory. For one day at least, Jimmy was the handsomest cat in the whole of Scotland.'

At a show held in Newcastle upon Tyne another cat of Jimmy-Hill-Shaw-type made his appearance, and, again it was his news value that had brought him on exhibition. This Woozie All-Black had saved the life of his owner when a fire broke out in her house; it was his plaintive mew into her ear that had aroused her in time to get help. The last line of the owner's tribute is quoted below:

> 'Except for Woozie's Mew,
> I might be dead and buried now,
> And quite forgotten too'.

In the past, cat shows were not such a serious business as they are today. Now cats must stand on their own four feet, completely unadorned. No pen can be ornamented, nor is any decoration at all allowed, and any attempt to beautify a cat, except by grooming, could mean disqualification. But in the early days of the Fancy after the use of straw had been discredited exhibitors were encouraged to put on a good show, and the sky was the limit. Judges gave useful tips on mixing colours to bring out the best points in the cat on show.

Frances Simpson said:

'Pink coloured ribbons are the most becoming to Blue kittens until their eyes have changed, then orange or yellow will be found more suitable. It is a mistake to tie very broad ribbons round your cat's neck when sending them to a show. I should choose a colour to match the eyes, about half an inch to three quarters in width. Tie in a neat bow and give a stitch in the centre, to prevent its coming untied. Don't leave too long ends. Orange is the most becoming colour for Blue cats.'

these cats' eyes should be emerald green or blue green only. A Silver Society was inaugurated in 1900. Another Society was then founded called the Silver and Smoke Persian Society, which broke up a few years later when Mrs Campion went to the U.S.A., but the Chinchilla Specialist Society did not come into being until 1919, after many storms had blown over the representatives of Silvers, Self Silvers, Shaded Silvers and Silver Tabbies.

'Chinnie', the Mother of all Chinchillas, was a familiar name to all Chinchilla breeders in 1882–5. She was bought originally for a guinea and for that amount was even sent on approval by rail. Many beautiful Chinchillas were descended from her, including Silver Lambkin, whose picture adorns so many old cat books.

Chinchillas increased in numbers very rapidly, and at the Cat Club show in 1903 there was a record entry in the male Silver cats class, which contained 22 cats, while the entry for females was 18. Lady Marcus Beresford's handsome 'Beetle' was a winner of a special prize.

The Silver Society also set standards for Silver Tabbies. The following was resolved: The colour of the Silver Tabby should be a pale clear silver, with distinct black markings, any brown or cream tinge to be considered detrimental, and the eyes should be orange or green. So breeders compromised about the colour and many excellent cats were exhibited at the Crystal Palace Show in 1902. Judges commented that the markings were too definite and some cats were nearly wholly silver. 'These pretty nondescript silvers, which are neither one thing or the other, should be disposed of as pets; but to enter them at our show in classes for tabbies is only throwing away money and risking the health of the animals' said one. Another judge wrote, 'competent judges agree that to breed regular, symmetrical and well-coloured markings is no easy task, for contrast is the grand point of a Silver Tabby. The head should be beautifully pencilled, the cheeks to possess double or treble swirls, the eyes should be out-lined by dark rims and on the forehead the lines should form a complete triangle.'

With the formation of new societies and the patronage of enthusiastic breeders at the Westminster Show in 1903, the entries in three open classes numbered twenty-seven, which showed that the numbers of Silver Tabbies were increasing rapidly.

Smoke Persians increased in the same way as Silver Tabbies and Silvers and Chinchillas had done. Smokes in full coat are magnificent cats, but when out of coat they appear very shabby and dishevelled. Because of these changes they were not good show cats. Writing of Smokes, Frances Simpson says:

'Smokes are comparatively speaking, one of the newer breeds of long-haired cats, and arose from the crossing of blues, blacks and silvers. No serious attempt was made to breed them until recently. If beauty and a hardy con-stitution count for much, they should be more popular than they are today'.

Orange Persians of the early days were really the Red Tabbies of today. Until 1894 the classification at the Crystal Palace was, 'Brown or Red Tabby, with or with-out white' and many oddly described cats came into these classes. When the specialist Society was founded the numbers at shows increased rapidly. At the Richmond Show in 1902 there were 13 entries in a combined class. Writing in a women's column about cats, Mrs Oxon remarked:

'It is difficult to imagine a more gorgeous colour than a really good orange lying full-length in the sun. There is, however, rather a prejudice against them, chiefly because some people insist in calling them 'sandy' or 'red', both of which names are quite misleading'.

The Cream or Fawn Persian became very fashionable at the beginning of the century. Again the breed got a boost when it found itself being taken care of by a specialist Society. The word 'cream' describes exactly what the desired tint should be, and pale creams were more attractive than ones of deeper hue. The principal points to be aimed at were avoidance of patches, streaks or tabby markings. It is a peculiarity of cream cats that their eyes are generally almond shaped, and set rather slanting in the head. Very famous Fawn or Cream Champions were the 'Heavenly Twins', bred by Miss Beal, whose famous cattery at Romaldkirk was situated 730 feet above sea level, and it was thought by breeders of the day that these cats flourished in the bitter climate. Northerners will beam kindly too on the hardy beauty and her stalwart Adonis 'Miriam of the Durhams' and 'Matthew of the Durhams', bred in Barnard Castle by Mrs Western. Though gently named there was nothing weak about the beautiful 'Devonshire Cream', owned by Mrs McLaren Morrison. Miss Beal agreed that 'one great point in favour of Creams was their hardiness.' They are also very useful to cross with other coloured cats like Blues or Silvers; they also cross well with Tortoiseshells.

Tortoiseshells are most fascinating creatures and Frances Simpson hinted that they were the most favoured of Persians by men judges, who invariably picked them out for Best in a mixed class. There should be three colours, black, red and yellow and they should be evenly distributed, with a 'blaze' on the face. The most famous of the old time Tortoiseshells was a beauty called 'Queen Elizabeth', who bit judges, stewards and attendants when she arrived by rail to attend the Westminster Show of 1899. But that did not prevent her from winning all before her then and afterwards. Looking through the old show catalogues it would appear that there were many more Tortoiseshells about in 1900 than there are today. Males were very rare even in those days, but there did emerge from Mrs Bignell's Cattery a very accommodating Blue, called 'The Duke of Kent', and he was considered a useful spouse for many of the otherwise passed over Tortoiseshells. This young cat produced excellent off-spring and he was greatly in demand.

Another addition to the Persians were the Tortoise-shell and Whites. Though not as popular as their tri-coloured relations, they had a certain brilliancy which was much admired. Harrison Weir, probably having the short-haired variety in mind, was quoted by Frances Simpson as having attributed to the colouring 'great artistic beauty'. Again these cats were lonely beauties, for none or few males turned up to their liking. At the Westminster Show of 1903 there was only one solitary entry in the Tortoiseshell-and-White class. Many photographs of these first Tortoiseshell-and-Whites, show cats with far too much white all over; though Harrison Weir says that noses should be white, this was the one spot where many nineteenth century show cats showed 'Any Other Colour'.

The magnificent Brown Tabbies that were exhibited many years ago were show cats in every sense of the word. Miss Simpson, the person whose name was most closely associated with the creation of interest in Brown Tabbies, says, of them:

'There is something so comfortable and homely about these dear brownies – they seem to have more intelligent and expressive countenances than any other cats, and I am firmly of the opinion that no Persian cats are so healthy and strong as Brown Tabbies. At the Crystal Palace Cat Show of 1902 the class was for brown or sable Tabby. I was judging, and, considering the mixed entries, I felt that markings must not be of the first importance.'

Miss Simpson added that better specimens of Brown Tabbies were produced in the North than in the South of England, and attributes this to the partiality of Brown Tabbies to cool climates. Spotted Tabbies were recognized and though few were entered in shows a few outstanding ones cropped up here and there from matings of Brown Tabbies and self-coloured Long-Hairs.

To a Persian Cat

Seeing you asleep in sweet content,
My mind runs back to centuries that were,
To ancestors that roamed the Orient
And left you all your elegance of fur.
No lovely lady meets the winter's gale
With warmer colour than your patterned red;
And that great plume that answers for a tail
Is all the grace that ever has been said.
Consistently you move through ordered days
Your captivating length of charm and style,
Unmindful of this sad old world's affrays,
And, in your way, preserve the things worthwhile.
Your right to aristocracy inheres
In beauty you have harboured through the years.

Christine Park Hankinson

5 The First Pedigree Short Hairs

Short-haired cats have always been associated with the ordinary, in feline life. Those of us who have lived for more than a few decades, and care to cast our minds back to our first association with cats, it will be to the well-fed and amiable nondescript short-haired cat that our thoughts will stray. Our memories of those days may be a little dim and we cannot, perhaps, recall whether our first pet cat was an all-black, a tabby, a ginger or white; that is not important; what is important is that it was of her virtues she was immortalized. Then a new star was seen in the cat lover's firmament and better days hovered in sight. A new generation was about to take over the affairs of cat. Harrison Weir saw great beauty in the old-fashioned cats and studied their points of excellence as no one had done hitherto. All the Short Hairs were allotted their own place in feline society and they appeared at shows 'all dressed up to kill'.

Mr Jung, one of the first known judges of Short-Hairs, said, by way of encouragement to the not fully convinced Short-Hair owner:

'The ordinary common garden cat suits my purpose; he is affectionate, he catches mice, and that is all I require. But how much more satisfactory it is to be able to say, my cat is blue-blooded, has an aristocratic pedigree, is handsome; he goes to shows, perhaps wins and he is still affectionate; he also catches mice as well as his brother of lower birth and less striking appearance. You must bear

Photo: Colour Library International Ltd.

Lu-Chu Siamese kittens bred by Mrs Yvonne Kite

Blue Persian Anonymous.
Study of an Exhibition Cat at
Newcastle Show, 1962 by
Dr Brian Eustace

International Champion
Trelystan Felspar.
Bred by Mrs John Paddon

Photo: Derek Folland

in mind that he does not require any daintier feeding. I consider it is always pleasanter in cat, dog, or horse to own a distinguished looking animal than an ill-bred, ungainly one, that neither pleases or satisfies the eye'.

So, Jung's reasoning and others as well inspired the new fanciers, and well-bred short-haired cats became fashionable. If the little companion of our hearth could boast of lineage he became an important being. The birth of the Cat Fancy elevated the Silver Tabby, the British Blue, the other colour Tabbies, Blacks, Whites and Tortoiseshells. The Silver Tabby seems to have been the first short-haired aristocrat of the new era of pedigree cats.

The famous Louis Wain, whose portrayal of cats brought him great fame, said of Silver Tabbies:

'Silver Tabbies, I must first class among the most aristocratic of the breeds. Fanciers will tell you how difficult it is to obtain a good one; either the tabby markings are not clear, nor sufficiently defined, the black is not dense enough, and the butterfly markings are not distinct, or the eyes are not of the correct colour. To get anything like a perfect type in silvers is a great feat, and is only the outcome of judicious mating. Among the winning males 'Champion Timmy' (already mentioned on page 28) stands out. He has won innumerable championships and First Prizes and is the property of Mrs Herring.'

Many important fanciers were alerted to the cries from the heart of so many intelligent cat lovers and several Long-Hair breeders acquired for their catteries one or two Silver Tabbies and other short-haired cats, but very few Champion Jimmys made their appearance. Cat Shows could never have gained momentum if Persian cats had not been the real show cats. Classes for Short-Hair cats were not well filled, and many fanciers complained about the inadequacy of the schedules.

A Mrs Elizabeth Judd wrote to a show manager in the following strain:

'The beautiful animal, the British cat is handicapped by

poor classification in comparison to Long-Hair. This is a great pity, because if a little encouragement were given the standards would improve'.

Nevertheless, it was not until the Foreign Short-Hairs appeared in increasing numbers that cat shows were a little better balanced.

Frances Simpson wrote:

'I would remark upon the absence of men who take up breeding cats as a hobby, and yet the short-haired variety is essentially a man's breed. They require very little grooming and attention compared to the long-haired variety'.

The beautiful British Blue was for many years confused with the Russian Blue. A great expert, writing of this breed said:

'For a long time we have called the self blues Russians. No doubt they, in the first instance, came from the East; but since they were imported into this country they have been mixed in a great measure with self blacks, and, in some cases with long-haired Blues, to get strong, short round heads so that at the present time we have very few pure-bred Russians in this country'.

Frances Simpson agreed that the crossing of British Blues and Russians had helped to produce the typical Blue. Then, in 1901, the class for Russians at the Crystal Palace show was dropped and instead it was called 'Short-haired Blues' and these should have round heads, and short legs, and a beautiful soft coat. As is always the case when looking for the best in self-coloured cats, white patches are completely out.

Mrs Carew-Cox, one of the first fanciers known, said she bought one of her first Blues after a show in 1889. Her standard calls for a 'short, close, glossy and silvery coat; sometimes it is woolly and furry. Short-haired blues existed in the North of Norway, and Iceland, and to enable these cats to exist in rigorous climates nature provided them with extra warm coats.' In the North of

Norway they were known as 'Canon Girdlestone's breed'. A British Cat Club, founded about 1902, had ardent supporters in Sir Claud and Lady Alexander, and this Club catered for, amongst other breeds, the British Blue. A trophy is offered annually at the National Cat Club Show at Olympia for the Best Blue Short Hair adult, presented by Lady Alexander; another of her trophies, the *Faygate Challenge Cup*, is awarded to the best *Blue-eyed White Short Hair*. Great confusion and many fresh dissertations were given about the combined Russians and Blues. Today this is simplified, for the establishment of the Russian Blue Cat Club gave Russians their real status. The British Cat Club did not draw up any special standards for the British Blue, the following definitions are clearly descriptive of the two breeds.

British Blue

Head – round and flat, with good space between the ears, which are small and well set on.

Russian Blue

Head longer in formation, with space between the ears, and well-tapered face; fairly round under the cheek bone, thin, falls away under the eye.

The eye colour in both was agreed as Deep Orange.

Amongst other British cats given pedigree status during the great days of the inauguration of the Fancy come the other coloured Tabbies, Self Colours and Tortoiseshells. The Brown Tabby is a very distinguished looking cat having the same markings as the Silver but, of course, the markings are on a brown background. It was permitted either green or orange eyes. Red Tabbies were not very common but some really good ones occasionally appeared. In *Cat Gossip* it was reported that a certain Mrs Oldfield was reputed to have bred a most magnificent Red. This cat should have made its debut at the Crystal Palace in 1903 but, in the course of show preparation it had to be bathed. So upset was it by these ablutions that it escaped from the house in wild pandemonium and was never seen again.

Glancing through old cat papers and magazines and books one is always saddened to hear of the tragic ending of the first pedigree cats. Very few indeed lived to old age, and though the motor car was not a hazard to be reckoned with, it is astounding the number of violent deaths that cats met with. But, of course, the greatest of all evils was the incidence of infectious disease, for which there were then no known remedies, and it was a case of survival of the fittest. But then humans were not favoured either and they too had to struggle against many of the ills that are so easily treated today.

A pure black, though commonplace it may appear, was one of the choicest of short-haired cats. But to be choice it had to have a very glossy rich coat, with green eyes, and no white should be anywhere in sight. They were not really popular as folk could not immediately be convinced of their importance. More popular was a plain white, which should have a shining coat and blue eyes. This type of cat has always looked a bit important, and more especially, if it could be framed with a litter of pure white kittens. Then it was a most appealing sight and a very rare picture it was. A short coat is very valuable in this breed, as very often they appear as half and half, half Persian and half Short-Hair; good shape and colour of eyes are both important features. A famous Short-Hair White of the long ago was Mrs Barker's 'Tyneside Lily', and she possessed a nice round face, good short coat and marvellous blue eyes.

Tortoiseshells and Tortoiseshells-and-Whites were recognised as separate breeds in the Short-Hairs as well as Long-Hairs, and were equally valuable and difficult to breed to the required standards. They should be a mixture of three colours, black, red and yellow; for this breed, white was a disqualification. In Harrison Weir's time these cats fetched very high prices, one famous 'Tortoise-shell tom-cat' was valued at 100 guineas. At the Crystal Palace Show of 1871 one Tortoiseshell male was shown and three Tortoiseshell and White. After 1873 pure Tortoise-shells disappeared completely from the show catalogues. Later when the Fancy was established they returned in small numbers and males were rarely ever seen. Harrison Weir quotes Cassell's *Natural History* to say that Tortoiseshells were common in Egypt and in the South of Europe. 'This I can believe', says Harrison Weir, 'as I think that it comes from a different stock than the usual short-hair cat, the texture of the hair being different, the form of tail also. A beautiful Tortoiseshell of the days of the infancy of the Fancy was one owned by Lady Alexander known as 'Samson'. However, though he lacked nothing in show points, he did not appear to be able to reproduce himself for a close search of records did not reveal any illustrious progeny. 'To breed Tortoiseshell he-cats,' commented Harrison Weir, 'I should use males of a self colour, such as either white, black or blue; and on no account any tabby, no matter the colour. What is wanted is patches of colour, not tiny streaks or spots; and I feel certain that, for those who persevere, there will be successful results.'

The Tortoiseshell-and-White again, as with Long-Hairs of this variety, should have in addition to black, red and yellow, white forelegs, breast, throat, lips, with a white blaze on the forehead. It should also have white on the lower half of their hind legs, a little on the nose, and the cushions of the feet white too. It is easy to see how difficult it would be to get this exact combination of colours. They were rare too, but not as rare as their counterpart in Long-Hairs, for judge Louis Wain must have seen a few when he identified Champion Ballochmyle Otter as the 'best he had penned', winner of 9 first prizes, the property of Lady Alexander.

Manx cats are one of the oldest of breeds. Tradition

has it that a rock in the Isle of Man named Spanish Rock got it's name from the memorable year of 1558 when the Spanish Armada went down, and that amongst the rescued cats were many tail-less cats which had been procured in the Far East. After the sinking, several of these cats swam to the shore and from this visitation the Manx Cat was first identified. Harrison Weir illustrated a prize winner at Crystal Palace shows in 1880, 1881, 1882, a brindled Tortoiseshell, without a particle of a tail. This was bred by a Mr Thomas, who kept the breed pure for many years. Miss Simpson said of Manx cats:

'They do not appeal to my sense of beauty; yet they are quaint little creatures, and one notices immediately the high hindquarters, which is so typical of the tail-less breed of cats, the few hairs which represent the spot where the tail should be. Manx cats should always be judged in a good, large, empty pen, and never in their own pens, or when held by a judge.'

She says that they are considered to be shy breeders and constantly the litter will consist of one kitten only. She also says that they are entirely fearless of dogs. A Manx Club was founded in 1901, and this club was responsible for a great improvement in the breed. An illustration of a pure black Manx, owned by Miss Samuels appeals to me very much, for it was known by the name of 'Golfsticks'.

It is recorded that the breed of cat known as the Abyssinian came from Africa about 1868. Many of the early cat historians said that the Abyssinian cat most nearly resembles the true Egyptian cat. These were formerly described as the 'bunny cat', because of the ticking of their coats which was very rabbit-like in markings and texture. According to Harrison Weir, the Abyssinians were known by a variety of names, some of which were, 'Russian, Spanish, Hare Cat, Rabbit Cat'. In his time they were very rare, and show schedules did not allot a breed class to them; they were shown under 'Any Other Colour'. The descriptions of the Abyssinian given by Harrison

Weir bore very little resemblance to the cat we know today as a true Abyssinian.

However, less than two decades later, Abyssinians had become more numerous, and in 1902 at the Crystal Palace there were no less than eleven Abyssinians on show. An impressive winner, with an impressive name was, 'The Little Bunny Teedle Tit'! Still, in spite of that good entry, Frances Simpson complained about show committees and judges and said that they neglected the Abyssinian breed. Another cause of complaint was 'the awful reports furnished by all-round reporters'.

H. C. Brooke, writing in *Cat Gossip*, said:

'There is much that is fascinating to learn about Abyssinians, and their beautiful colours and arrangements of markings should be studied. To the search for something new we owe the beautiful Siamese. Will no one pay any attention to the other varieties of foreign breeds who have come to us from distant lands? They are well worth further study, and the addition of more foreign cats at our shows would be very interesting and instructive.'

The Cat Show

To see them is to Love them,
To watch them is to admire them,
Sleek, graceful creatures they are.

To describe them is to attempt the impossible.
Shining, lustrous, poised, regal,
words are but meagre praises.

Haughty Persians,
Gleaming Siamese,
Manx, Abyssinians, Short Hairs,
unassailable all
With the speed of Mercury,
the grace of the fawn,

the shyness of the coquette,
the poise of the aristocrat,
the litheness of the panther,
and the wariness of the jungle.

To see them is to love them;
to watch them is to admire them;
to do them justice
is beyond the poor powers of their adorers.

                              Marguerite L. Nolan
                              (From *Sophisti-cats*)

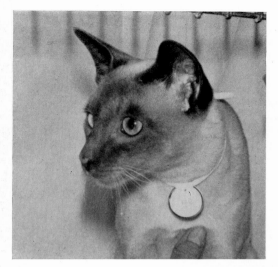

Premier Whitehaugh Blue Nylon. Bred by Mrs Challoner; owner Mrs I. North

Premier Cathiss Gypsella. Owner Mrs K. Vickers

Amberley Deborah.
Owners, Mr and Mrs
Wilson

Photo: Dr Brian Eustace

Hawthorn kittens

6 *The First Siamese Cats*

We all have our different theories and beliefs about the origin of the Siamese Cat. Some are more romantic than others. Sir Compton Mackenzie, writing in his introduction to Phil Wade's book *The Siamese Cat* in 1934, says he does not agree with Phil Wade who attributes the origin of the Siamese Cat to Egypt, but prefers to suppose that the qualities that distinguish it from other cats are due to its having no connection with the Egyptian or European wild cat or the Persian. With this view most of us are in agreement, but we do not quite accept what he offered instead, that, 'The Siamese cat is a selected and inbred variant of the Malay jungle cat. It is in fact a semi-albino, and it is noticeable that the same kind of colouring has been produced by selection and inbreeding in the Jersey cow.' No! though this theory might be correct, I reject it. Instead I prefer what was presented to us by M. Oldfield Howey in his book, *The Cat in the Mysteries of Religion and Magic*, who places the Siamese Cat as a descendant of the Sacred Cat of Burma, one of The Temple Cats of a bygone age.

'Obviously the cats which sat upon the statues of the gods were sacred animals belonging to the Temple. It is clear that they were well-fed felines, not hungry strays. They were in fact, highly venerated, and had their part to play in the aspect of religion accepted by this ancient people, for when a human being who had attained a certain degree of holiness died, the cat acted as the host of his soul for the rest of his natural life. Only by this means could the departed soul gain paradise, as none was privileged to attain this coveted reincarnation as a sacred cat within the holy temple without the express sanction of the presiding goddess. Even today (1930) Burmese and Siamese believe that their beautiful, sacred cats enshrine the spirits of the dead, and with this in mind they introduce them into their religious ritual. Years ago when a member of the royal house of Siam was buried, one of his favourite cats used to be entombed alive with him. The roof of the burying place was designed with small holes piercing it, and if the cat succeeded in escaping through one of these, the priests knew that the soul of the prince had passed into its body, as they conducted it to the Temple with appropriate honours.

'Ancestor worship is still an impelling force in Oriental countries. It was probably in order to show reverence to the departed monarch that when the young King of Siam was crowned in 1926, a white cat was carried by the Court Chamberlains in the procession to the Throne Room. Along with the sacred cat were borne a grindstone, symbolizing firmness, a gherkin for happiness, and grain for prosperity'.

Mrs Cran, an authority on Siamese cats, writing in *Cat Gossip*, has described what is known as the Temple Mark. 'Two distinct markings may be found on the backs of some highly bred Siamese which are said to be the distinguishing feature of The Temple Cat.'

Attempts to trace the name of the God who left his shadow for ever on the descendants of the Siamese Cat, have not been successful. Nevertheless, to Mrs Cran, for this delightful anecdote, we give our grateful thanks.

However, it is well established that Siamese cats were in existence for over 200 years before being introduced into England, and that they were solely the companions of Kings in the Royal City of Bangkok; but many things about their origin are obscure. From many references to the Temple Cat, which was believed to have been called the Sacred Cat of Burma, it is agreed that the Siamese Cat was descended from this older breed. From the descriptions given, the cat known in France today as the Birman Cat is a true Temple Cat, and for this reason many fanciers will read with interest the efforts made by the Hon. Russell Gordon to collect authentic information about the 'Birmans'. It was while serving as an English Officer during the Burmese War in 1885 that opportunities arose for a close study of this species.

He described the Temple of Lao-Tsun as 'one of the greatest marvels of the East – situated to the East of Lake Incaougji between Magaoung and Sembo, in an almost desert region of immense peaks and chaotic labyrinths, it offers a barrier of insurmountable walls. Here there existed in 1898, the last kittahs (priests) and as a most extraordinary favour I was permitted to see and observe them and their sacred animals. Following the rebellion and the English occupation at the base of the Bhamo, we had to protect the kittahs against a Brahmin invasion, and we saved them from certain massacre and pillage. Their Lama-kittah received me and presented me with a plaque representing the Sacred Cat at the feet of a bizarre deity, whose eyes were made of two long sapphires'.

Gordon described these Temple Cats as 'being like the Siamese in colouring, but has white toes on all four feet, long hair, and magnificent bushy tails which are usually carried over their backs in squirrel fashion. Their eyes were intensely blue, deep and melancholy-gentle when at rest, but wild and fiery if angered'.

This description must be very valuable in giving the Sacred Cat of Burma his proper setting.

Harrison Weir included in his first record a survey of the Siamese Cat. He was very much intrigued with the newcomer, who was a complete outsider to the newly-established world of pedigree cats. This Royal Cat of Siam was different from the other short hair cats, in style, type, colouring and bearing. Though Harrison Weir never possessed a Siamese cat, it did not prevent him from making a close study of this breed as an observer with a very open mind.

His search for knowledge of the Siamese Cat took him to the homes of the most important cat lovers in England at the time. Those associated with the first imports were mostly in the foreign service of the colonial empire or were generals domiciled abroad, whose high style of living brought them into contact only with class cats. It would appear that these cats had an immediate appeal and many attempts were made to secure them. The solitary little pair that arrived in England in 1886 were brought in by Mr Gould, the consul-general in Bangkok, and were immediately acclaimed as Top Cats. A few years later, Mrs Vyvyan brought in a few more and very slowly, and after many losses, the breed was established. Mrs Vyvyan spoke of the difficulty in getting more specimens, 'They are procured only as a great favour, after much delay and great difficulty'. We find that these cats require a great deal of care, unless they live in the country, and become hardy through being constantly out of doors. The kittens are difficult to rear unless they are born in the late spring, when the weather is warm. We have lost several kittens mostly from worms. They are interesting and delightful pets. But, owing to their delicacy and the great care they require, no one, unless a real cat lover, should attempt to keep them; they cannot with safety be treated as common cats'. Mrs Vyvyan was one of the founder members of the first Siamese Cat Club.

From Mr Brennand, Harrison Weir collected more information about his foreign friends. 'I have heard a little more regarding the Siamese cats from Miss Walker, the daughter of General Walker, who brought over one male and three females. It seems that only the pure breed is kept at the King of Siam's palace, and that these cats are very difficult to procure, for in Siam it took three different gentlemen of great influence, three months before they could get any'.

Another of the people concerned in the attempts to establish the first Siamese breed was Lady Dorothy Nevill, but she was unsuccessful having lost all her stock. Harrison Weir says, 'Lady Dorothy Nevill informed me that those which belonged to her were imported from Siam and presented by Sir R. Herbert of the Colonial Office; the late Duke of Wellington imported the breed, also Mr Scott of Rotherfield. Lady Nevill thought them exceedingly docile and domestic, but delicate in their constitution; although her ladyship kept one for two years, another over a year, but eventually all died of the same complaint, that of worms, which permeated every part of their body'.

But though Lady Dorothy was unsuccessful with Siamese she kept and bred many Long-Hairs.

Though the high mortality of Siamese cats in those early years was most disconcerting, many survived and the breed finally became established.

At the Crystal Palace quite a few were shown from the year 1886–90, but these were not in classes by themselves but entered in Any Other Variety. It was once reported that a cat named 'King Of Siam', imported straight from the Royal Palace, was exhibited and was awarded 'Very Highly Commended'.

Harrison Weir recounts that in one of those early catalogues he found that there were 'fifteen females and only four males, and some of those were not entire; and I have always understood that the latter was not allowed to be exported, and were only procured by those so fortunate, as a most extraordinary favour, as the King of Siam is most jealous of keeping the breed entirely in Siam'.

But though valuable and rare as the Siamese cats were, in the next few years they were brought in in great numbers to England.

Frances Simpson, writing nearly two decades later, collected much valuable information from people who had previously been interviewed by Harrison Weir. These were now of a more permanent record, for at the time of the publication of *The Book of the Cat*, dedicated to Harrison Weir, Siamese cats were gradually becoming acclimatized and their popularity was firmly established. Also, the Siamese Cat Club had been founded and show cats and show points had become important. There was great confusion and controversy about the two types, Chocolate-Pointed and Seal-Pointed, and even in 1903 the doyens of the Fancy rushed to *Fur and Feathers* to air their complaints. 'One great object of the Siamese Cat Club is to encourage the distinct breeding of the Royal Cat of Siam and also of the Chocolate Cat of Siam – both beautiful in their own way, but recognized as distinct breeds'. After much more deliberation these pioneers signed their names as, A. Forestier Walker, Jean A. Spencer, May Robinson, L. Parker-Brough, S. E. Backhouse, Constance Carew Cox. Presumably this group were the first fanciers to seriously consider colour variations in the breed.

Another source of conflicting opinions between new breeders was the correct type of tail which the ideal Siamese cat should possess. Many fanciers tried to preserve the 'kink', and Mrs Forestier Walker, who was a cat judge and one of the founders of the Siamese Cat Club said, 'The tails are sometimes straight, which is not a fault; but a knot or kink in the tail is a peculiarity of the breed, and therefore desirable. In England it has been asserted that this is a defect, but in Siam it is highly prized, and cats from the royal palaces which have been given by the King as presents of value to important people have had this distinction. In the East, a cat with a kinked tail fetches a higher price'.

It is certain that Champion Wankee, owned by Mrs Robinson had a pronounced kink, and many important cats exhibited in the first shows were similarly affected. It is written that, 'Mrs Robinson's Wankee, was the first Siamese to win the title of Champion. He was bred in Hong-Kong, his mother, Nims, being a stolen palace kitten. Wankee was six months old when he arrived in

England, born in September 1895. He won over thirty prizes. He had a decided kink, looking, in fact, as though his tail had been caught in a door. His eyes had no sign of a squint, but this is not important. On the question of kinks, the Siamese Cat Club remains neutral'.

From every possible source the information about the first Siamese cats points to their delicacy. Very few pioneer breeders found that the breeding of Siamese cats was easy. Miss Armitage writes for Frances Simpson, 'I have very few Siamese cats at present; I lost so many beautiful ones last year that I think I made a mistake in not having their skins made into mats. I have now a lovely daughter of 'Cora' and Champion Wankee, aged nine months. When she was a few hours old I put her to be fostered by our English garden cat, who makes her headquarters in the greenhouse. The kitten has never had a day's illness. She leads a wild life, catching birds and mice, and nibbling the tips off the ferns – much to our gardener's annoyance'.

She encouraged several breeders to harden the Siamese kittens by giving them to a healthy common cat to foster. Miss Forestier Walker also advocated the fostering of Siamese kits to make the breed stronger.

The charming Lady Marcus Beresford, who founded the Cat Club, included in her cat entourage many Siamese cats, and it would seem that she had a fair share of success. She wrote for Frances Simpson, 'I have never had any trouble or anxiety with Siamese cats. They are dear, gentle, friendly little people, so clever and so attractive. I have never seen any I admired so much. They had many fine healthy litters, scattered about now amongst various friends'.

Mrs Parker Brough, one of the founder members of the Siamese Cat Club, says, amongst many other things, 'This breed is certainly the noisiest, least dignified, most intelligent and most active of all cats. They are dog-like in their nature, and can be easily taught to turn back-somersaults, and to retrieve, and in the country, take long walks like a terrier. If they think it is meal-time and they fancy themselves neglected, they cry like children. The points of the perfect royal cat lie in the eyes, which should be a most perfect blue, and the contrast between the seal-brown of the paws, mask, and tail and the white or cream of the rest of the body, which should not be disfigured by bars or blotches'.

Miss Cochrane, a vice-president and founder member of the Siamese Cat Club and also a judge besides being a very prominent exhibitor at the first shows, regretted the short life enjoyed by so many Siamese cats. 'Alas! that these little companions to whom we are permitted to become so deeply attached should be only lent to brighten our weary way for so short a period! 'To-To' was always very delicate, and after lying at death's door on several occasions she finally entered in; with her very last breath she crept into my arms to die'.

Siamese cats appeared at shows in England in mixed classes almost from the date of their arrival in the country, and with the commencement of the Cat Fancy as we know it today, they soon found their level with classes for Siamese only.

Frances Simpson says, in her introductory paragraph on Siamese Cats, 'I have often remarked at our cat shows that strangers in the Fancy will enquire and ask to be directed to the Siamese class, and many and varied are the exclamations of surprise and admiration expressed by them on seeing for the first time, a row of Siamese cats seated in their pens. Nor is it always necessary to direct visitors to the Siamese classes, for generally these animals will betray their whereabouts by the unique tone of their voice, which is distinguishable at a great distance.'

The most famous of all local shows was the Sandy Show, or to give it its full title, 'The exhibition of the Sandy and District Floral and Horticultural Show'. In 1894 a cat section was introduced, and cats were exhibited in company with cage birds, rabbits and dogs. This seems to have been the most permanent of all shows for it went on for many years and has been in existence almost down to our own time. Siamese were exhibited at the first cat show held by the Sandy promoters, and were never omitted from the classification. A very popular feature of this show was the Ring Class, which took the form of a parade of cats on stout satin ribbons. Many tales of amusement have emanated from the Sandy Show including the one when a cat tried to escape and the judge imprisoned it in her long, flowing skirt!

Though many proud Siamese breeders felt it incumbent on them to present their cats at shows, many losses were sustained because of the spread of infection and the weakness of the breed. Still, when one views these early catalogues, the number of Siamese exhibited at all-breed shows was nearly as large as today. There were many champions too, as there are today, making long journeys to be shown. A note in *Cat Gossip* says, 'Mrs Chapman's "Wally Pug" has crossed the Irish Channel to visit his first English Cat Show. He returned home well contented with his three VHC's'.

Miss Armitage sustained many losses through infection contracted at shows. Her famous 'Sam Sly' returned from a Manchester Show, festooned with honours and medals, but only arrived home in time to place his head on a pillow and die. Mrs Parker Brough's 'Koschka', famed for the most beautiful blue eyes ever seen, died two days after Westminster Show in 1900. Miss Armitage says later of another of her acquisitions, 'My "Royal Siam", who came from the royal palace, is a splendid specimen. He has never ailed anything since I have had him. I have never placed him at stud but have allowed a few selected friends to visit him, and bring their queens. Neither have I ever exhibited him, for he is far too precious a pet to be allowed to run risks.' So seriously had the threat of disease affected many Siamese breeders that entries fell off and at the Westminster Show in 1903 the Siamese classes were cancelled because of no entries. But this caution was only temporary, for nothing could dampen the enthusiasm of breeders and soon they came back again in greater numbers than ever.

How different would things have been for these precious cats and their adoring humans if they had lived today and had the advantages of inoculation against Feline Infective Enteritis and the various forms of distemper that can now be isolated! But nothing could stem the growth of the popularity of Siamese cats. Soon, with the blessings of the English Cat Fancy, they made a glorious entry into the New World. In 1900, American writer Helen M. Winslow, in her book, *Concerning Cats*, says of the Siamese, 'The Royal Cat of Siam is a short-haired cat, yet widely different from other short-haired varieties. They are extremely pretty, with blue or amber coloured eyes by day which grow brilliant at night. These cats also frequently have the kink in the tail, and sometimes a strong animal odour, although this is not disagreeable. The head is rather longer than the ordinary cat's, tapering off sharply toward the muzzle, the forehead flat and receding, and the eyes more slanting towards the nose than the American cat's. The form should be slender, and the feet oval. The body is of a bright, uniform colour, and the legs, feet and tail are usually black.'

Mrs Clinton Locke, one of the first American women to start a cattery had innumerable cats, and even before the turn of the century she had acquired a choice pair of Siamese cats called 'Siam' and 'Sally Ward' and from these she bred 'Calif' and 'Bangkok'. 'Siam' was a big, round-faced substantial-looking gentleman, but 'Chom', his son, bred by Mrs Cronise of San Francisco, was quite as elegant-looking and refined as many of our show cats today, his only blemish being a shortish, kinked tail.

In very early days too, mention was made of a Dr H. L. Hammond, of Connecticut, who specialized in collecting rare Australian cats. Amongst these were two of great

value, known as 'Columbia' and 'Tricksey'. These won
prizes whenever shown and were definitely Siamese in
type, being descended from the first imported Siamese to
Australia about 1895. Dr and Mrs Hammond were
extremely devoted to these two beautiful cats and told
many anecdotes about their antics and behaviour. The
depth of their slumbers was very Siamese-like in character.
The doctor said, 'They have spells of sleeping when
nothing has power to disturb them, but when they awake
they are immediately bright and high-spirited.' These
observations are very interesting for it is well-known that
Siamese cats will certainly out-sleep all others, and I,
myself, have noticed that when I suddenly went into a
room where the Burmese, Silver Tabby and Siamese were
sleeping, the first to be alerted was the Silver Tabby, who
never missed the slightest human sound. Next to rouse
herself was the Burmese, and last came my Siamese. The
Siamese certainly knew how to relax and when she went
to bed she went there to sleep. Sometimes she would have
to be touched to make her wake up. On first acquaintance
with Siamese they are often mistakenly dubbed as 'deaf'.
But their sense of smell is almost uncanny and the keen
nostrils of a Siamese can penetrate through closed and
sealed doors, especially if food is in the offing.

Even today, Siamese and Blue Persians are the only
two breeds that can attract sufficient numbers to hold a
specialist show.

The Siamese Cat Club was founded in 1902, and twenty-
one years later the first Championship Siamese Cat Show
was inaugurated. The show was held at the Pilbeach
Gardens Hall, Kensington, on September 24th, 1924. Only
two judges officiated. The first was Mrs Cran, a well-
known writer, whose gardening books brought her great
fame in the early thirties, and who was also an important
contributor to Cat Gossip. References by her to Temple
Cats are already quoted in this chapter. The other judge
was Miss Lea, whose name was for many years associated

with the National Cat Club as pre-show registrar, and she had interests in other breeds of cats besides Siamese, being the first secretary of the Orange, Cream, Fawn and Tortoiseshell Society. With these two important judges handing out the honours the winners at this first show were of no mean calibre.

Altogether there were over 90 exhibits, which included a litter class of 6. The two Challenge Certificates were won by Miss C. Fisher, with her Seal-Pointed Siamese, Ruakina of Cornwall and Belinda of Cornwall. There were also Chocolate-Pointed exhibits, but no Challenge Certificates were awarded for these.

Many people associated with the Siamese Cat Club during its infancy and growth are remembered by Memorial trophies which are still possessed by the Club and these are handed out at the Annual Show, which has now had its 36th birthday. The Vyvyan-Walker Memorial Cup, presented by Mrs J. Swann in memory of her two illustrious aunts, is awarded to the *Seal-Point adult with palest coat and most oriental eye*. The Mary Robinson Trophy for the *Best Pair*, commemorates the secretary who kept the club alive during the difficult years of World War One, when the foundations of the Western World rocked and it seemed as if our civilization might end. Membership fell to the lowest ever, a solitary 19. She was secretary until her death in 1923. This award was won in 1958 by two Seal-Points, Hillcross Sheng and Hillcross Sapphire, and as the trophy cannot be won outright the breeder received as a memento, a silver medal in a leather case. The Phil Wade Trophy is awarded for the exhibit which has *Best Condition and Easiest to Handle*. Phil Wade was one of the most important pre-war chairmen, and the late Mrs K. R. Williams, a past secretary too, dedicated her first book to Phil Wade and Cyril Yates in these words: 'This book is dedicated to the memory of Phil Wade, who did so much for Siamese cats and to Cyril Yates whose life was devoted to Cats Of All Breeds'.

Particularly valuable now is the Doneraile Trophy, presented by Capt. Williams, for this too will always remind exhibitors of a colourful personality whose writings about Siamese cats brought her into the top flight as a fancier. The tragedy of her violent death in a car crash was a bitter blow to the many Siamese cat lovers who had had the benefit of her advice and help. She was returning from a Show in Halifax and was identified by her Cat Club papers, the principal being her unfinished judging book, wherein her last words written were of Siamese cats.

Except for the break caused by World War Two, the annual shows have been a feature of interest to Siamese breeders. The names of Mrs Hindley and Mrs Kent will always be associated with having done so much to keep the breed alive during the war.

Frances Simpson, in her concluding notes on Siamese cats, published in 1903, summarized her thoughts as follows: 'I do not believe that Siamese cats will ever become common in England, for many reasons. These cats are expensive to purchase, difficult to rear, and fanciers are afraid to risk them in the show pen; but in spite of these drawbacks, I think, as time goes on, and the Siamese club extends its labours, we shall see and hear more of these really curious creatures, for what we call the Royal Cat bears no resemblance to any other cat, and the distinguishing difference being so great, tend to make the breed one of our best show cats and a clear class to itself, for the Siamese of the purest blood should not be crossed with other cats. We have heard of 'Any Other Colour Siamese' but these cats of varied hue claiming to be Siamese are but the offspring of a cross. We have been told of black, and blue and tabby Siamese; but the fanciers of Siamese look askance at these freaks, and feel that it is worse than useless to attempt to produce any other variety than that which we have learned by custom to designate: The Royal Cat of Siam.'

In alphabetical order below are a few of the first names to appear in the Siamese Cat Register:

1. Aguthea. M. Parents unknown, imported, born 1894. Owner M. A. Steven.
2. Ah Choo. F. Sire Tiam O'Shian III. Dam. Polyphema. Born 3/5/1900. Owner, Mrs M. Robinson.
3. Ahlan. M. Sire, Ming; Dam, Bhopal Ranee, born 9/8/1912. Owner, Mrs M. Robinson.
4. Ahmatt. M. Parents unknown, imported, born about 1908. Owner, Mrs Lowry.
5. Alector. M. Parents unknown, born 14/4/1906, Owner, Mrs Trotter.
6. Ampal. M. Parents unknown. Owner Miss Martin (Won a 2nd prize, Manchester 1897).
7. Ampat. M. Parents unknown, born Sept. 1893. Owner Lt. Colonel A. C. Alexander (Won 2nd prize Crystal Palace 1895).

Skipping a few to find a familiar name we come to:
13. Appah. M. Sire Mon Dek, Dam, Putch. Born 20/3/1920. Owned and bred by Mrs Hindley.

7 What's in a Name?

What's in a name? Before the arrival of the pedigree cat, much indeed. The old-fashioned cats could not trace their lineage, or boast of an imposing pedigree, so it was by their names that they were mostly immortalized. Those with commonplace names like Peg or Peter made little impact on cat biographers; except of course in odd cases like that of Louis Wain, who made the name Peter famous by his drawings for the *Illustrated London News* of December, 1890. But on the whole, pretty, impressive or uncommon names were a ticket-of-fame to nineteenth century cats. Many of the important cat owners, seeing into the future, created an air of mystery and glamour by giving their cats high-sounding and distinctive names.

Cat's Who's Who of a Bygone Age
The Most Noble, the Archduke Rumpelstilzchen,
Marcus Macbum, Earl Tomlefnagne, Baron Raticide,
Waowhler and Scratch and Rumpel.

This illustrious cat belonged to Robert Southey poet-laureate. Few cat lovers will not have read in some cat book or other, the letter he wrote to his friend, when he announced the death of his adored cat.

'My much loved cat Rumpel of the many names, was found dead today, after a long and happy life. There should be a court-mourning in Catland and your pet cat should wear a band of crepe, in military style round one of his forepaws, as a becoming mark of respect. I believe we are each and all, servants included, more sorry for his loss than any of us would like to confess'.

Childebrand – Merovingian

This cat was a splendid cat of common kind, tawny and striped with black, one of Théophile Gautier's cats. Gautier, the French writer and poet, did not name his cats without giving the matter great thought, and from Frances Cashel-Hoey's translation of Campfleury's book on cats we read with interest Gautier's discourse about suitability of names.

'Childebrand at once reveals a deep design of flouting Boileau, whom I did not like then, but have since become reconciled to. Childebrand is a very fine name indeed, Merovingian, mediaeval, and Gothic, and vastly preferable to Agamemnon, Achilles, Ulysses, or any Greek name whatever. Romanticism was the fashion of my early days; I have no doubt the people of classical times called their cats Hector, Ajax or Patroclus'.

Madame Théophile

This 'Madame Théophile' was another of Gautier's cats. This was the name given to 'a red cat with a white breast, a pink nose and blue eyes, whom I called by the name Madame Théophile because we were on such terms of close intimacy'. He tells a very amusing story of this cat and a friend's parrot. 'Madame Théophile crept nearer and nearer almost imperceptibly; her pink nose quivered, her eyes were half closed, her contractile claws moved in and out of their velvet sheaths, slight thrills of pleasure ran along her backbone at the idea of the meal she was going to have. Such novel and exotic food excited her appetite. The parrot, seeing her danger said in a bass voice, "As tu déjeuné, Jacquot?" The utterance so terrified the cat that she sprang backwards, crashing into china and ornamental glass. Observers of the physiognomy of Madame Théophile, interpreted her growl to mean: "This is not a bird, it is a gentleman; it talks". After a few more shrieks from the parrot the cat took refuge under the bed, and nothing would induce her to show herself again. The parrot had won the first round'.

Don Pierrot-de-Navarre

This was another of Gautier's cats, and again, this handsome fellow was named as a kitten, Pierrot, because of his immaculate white coat. When he grew up his name was magnified 'to make him appear more majestic, with a sense of grandee-ism' into Don Pierrot-de-Navarre. Don Pierrot-de-Navarre was a cultured and remarkable cat, liking books and music with the same relish as his illustrious owner. But, according to Gautier, he had an aversion to late nights.

'Pierrot was as strict as a concierge in his notions of the proper hour for all good people to return to their homes. He did not approve of anything later than midnight. In those days we had a little society among friends, which we called "The Four Candles" – the light in our place of meeting restricted to four candles. Sometimes the talk became so animated that I forgot all about time, and twice or three times Pierrot sat up for me until two o'clock in the morning. After a while, however, my conduct in this respect, displeased him and he retired to bed without me. I was touched by this mute protest against my dissipation, and henceforth came home regularly at twelve o'clock. Nevertheless, Pierrot cherished the memories of my offence for sometime; he waited to test the reality of my repentance, but when he was convinced that my conversion was sincere, he deigned to restore me to his good graces, and resume his nocturnal post in the anteroom'.

Seraphita of Balzac Swedenborgian

Seraphita was Pierrot's sweetheart, being of the same race and colour. In Gautier's estimation she was the most georgeous, most luxurious, most aristocratic, most elegant cat he had ever seen. She was also of a most dreamy and contemplative disposition. She was very full too, of her own importance. She had one antipathy; though caresses were agreeable to her, when anyone touched her she 'instantly effaced all trace of contact for she could not endure to be tumbled'. Perfumes to her were very agreeable, and she would stick her nose into bouquets of roses, or bite anything scented with little spasms of joy. 'Such was Seraphita' said Gautier, 'and never did cat more amply justify a poetic name.'

Enjolras and Gavroche and Eponine

These were the three black offspring of Pierrot and Seraphita. Enjolras was the handsomest of the three and was 'remarkable for his broad, leonine head and full whiskers, strong shoulders and a superb feathery tail'. About Gavroche his owner said,

'He was wonderfully active, and his twists and twirls and tumbles were most comic. He was of a Bohemian temperament, and fond of low company'.

Eponine was more graceful and slender than her two brothers. Of Eponine the owner wrote:

'Eponine's intelligence, fine disposition and sociability led her to being elevated to the dignity of a person. This dignity conferred on her the right to eat at table like a person, and not in a corner on the floor, from a saucer like an animal. Eponine had a chair by my side at breakfast and dinner, but in consideration of her size she was privileged to place her forepaws on the table'.

As these cats were born at the time when Victor Hugo's *Les Misérables* was a new masterpiece, they were named after the personages so commonly referred to in conversations at the time.

Micetto

Micetto, another cat very attractively named, was the cat given by the Pope as a gift to his friend, Chateaubriand. This cat inspired him to write, in his memoirs, many eulogisms on cats. 'I love in the cat,' wrote Chateaubriand, 'that independent and most ungrateful temper which prevents it from attaching itself to anyone; the indifference with which it passes from the salon to the housetop.' Many cat lovers of today would not consider these references complimentary to the cat, disagreeing entirely with these sentiments, preferring to believe that cats do attach themselves to humans, and would indeed be affected by a change from high living to low life. Certainly, my first little Siamese cat, Ming, always clung to me as her life-saver, and our home was to her a Garden of Eden. Ming would find nothing relevant to her state in Chateaubriand's eulogisms.

Fromentin

Fromentin was one of the 30 cats with whom the French writer Paul de Kock, shared his home. This Fromentin lived to a very old age and references to him were given place in many of his writings. Many cats of that age were named Fromentin of one sort or another, Menty being a cut-down favoured by personal friends.

Moumette Blanche and Moumette Chinoise

These two adorable cats figured in the writings of Pierre Loti. Handsomely named they could not easily be forgotten.

Gaudalquiver

This Spanish named cat was one of the pets of Harrison Weir, and it was said of him by his owner that he knew the days of the week. His favourite food, horse flesh, was delivered every day of the week except on Sundays, and Gaudalquiver sat at the doorstep every day, waiting for the sweetly-scented parcel to be delivered, but, on a Sunday he never left the parlour and the comfort of an open fire which he shared with his master.

Lillah and Zillah and Zeno and Lulu and The Colonel

These friendly cats were Harrison Weir's 'Garden Cats', and they had many duties with regard to the keeping down of vermin and maurauders. But, they were very domesticated, always willing to abandon their tasks when they were invited to go for a walk. Harrison Weir related how much he looked forward to these outings with his cats and how he was able to identify each cat by its different traits. Zillah was the friendly one, Zeno was the sulky one who wanted the place nearest her owner, and often went away if she had to play second fiddle to Lulu, and The Colonel was the most distinguished looking of the gathering. Harrison Weir reported that they all had sad endings, being trapped in poacher's wires set for rabbits.

Tacitus, the 'lone and lorn'

Helen Winslow's cats must take their bows wherever late nineteenth century cats are on parade. These cats were all specially named so that their importance could never be overlooked. I find that Tacitus was about the most human of her many cats. He carried on his person many scars and bruises. Wrote Helen Winslow:

'He had a habit of dodging in and out of the front door, which was heavy, and which sometimes flung together before he was well clear of it. As a consequence, a caudal appendage with two broken joints was one of his disfiguring features. Besides a broken tail, he had ears which bore the marks of many a hard-fought battle. But I loved him, and judging from the disconsolate and long-continued wailing with which he filled the house whenever I was away, my affection was not unrequited'.

Pretty Lady and her son, Mr McGinty

Pretty Lady was the apple of the eye of Miss Winslow. Pages upon pages have been written about this pretty Maltese cat. She lived to be nine years old and had ninety-three kittens. Her two best known kittens were Mr McGinty and her adopted one Black Bobbie. When Pretty Lady died her epitaph was written thus:

Requiescat in pace, my Pretty Lady. I wish all your sex had your gentle dignity, and grace and beauty, to say nothing of your faithfulness and affection.

Pompanita, the Good

Yes, his name describes him, and Miss Winslow amplifies it further. 'Pampanita the Good has all the virtues of a good cat, and absolutely no vices. He loves us all and loves all other cats as well. As for fighting, he emulates the example of that veteran who boasts that during the war he might always be found where the shot and shell was thickest – under the ammunition waggon.

Lady Betty and Plain Jane

Miss Winslow says that Lady Betty was the most aristocratic cat of her age 'for she kept a wet nurse. Poor Jane of the commoner strain did the needful, and she dismissed her plebeian infants in favour of Lady Betty's aristocrats. Four fluffy little Angoras names, Chin, Chilla, Buffie and Orange Pekoe, made up the new family. And Jane, wet nurse and waiting-maid, had to keep as busy as the old woman who lived in the shoe. Jane it was who looked after the infants when Lady Betty wished to leave the house. Jane it was who must scrub the furry quartette until their silky fur stood up in bunches the wrong way all over their chubby little sides; Jane must sleep with them at nights, and be ready to furnish sustenance at any moment of day or night; and, above all, Jane must watch them anxiously and incessantly in waking hours, uttering those little protesting murmurs of admonition which mother cats deem so necessary toward the proper training of kittens.'

Mutilator

This was the cat of the *New York Sun* Office who lived in the last century. Many American tales are linked with this cat and Mr Dana, who told this story to Miss Winslow, vouched for its veracity by quoting a famous phrase, 'If you see it in the *Sun*, it is so'.

'The *Sun* Office cat is a variation of the common domestic cat, of which but one family is known to science.

The habitat of the species is in Newspaper Row; its lair is the *Sun* buildings, its habits are nocturnal and it feeds on discarded copy and anything else of a pseudo-literary nature upon which it can pounce. In dull times it can subsist upon a meagre diet of telegraphic brevities, police court paragraphs, and city jottings; but when the universe is agog with news, it will exhibit the insatiable appetite which is its chief distinguishing mark of difference from the common felis domestica.'

After these really interesting remarks on the *Sun* cat in general Dana then describes the Mutilator and how he got his name.

'Grown to cat-hood he is a creditable specimen of his family, with beryl eyes, beautiful striped fur, showing fine mottlings of mucilage and ink, a graceful and aspiring tail, an appetite for copy unsurpassed in the annals of his race, and a power and perseverance in vocality, chiefly exercised in the small hours of the morning, that, together with the appetite referred to, have earned for him the name of Mutilator. Up to the age of one year the Mutilator made its lair in the inside office with the Snake Editor, until a tragic ending came to their friendship. During a fortnight's absence of the office cat on important business, the Snake Editor cultivated the friendship of three cockroaches, whom he debauched by teaching them to drink beer spilled upon the desk for this purpose. On the night of the cat's return the three bugs had become disgracefully intoxicated, and were reeling round the desk beating time with their legs to a rollicking catch song by the Snake Editor. Before the muddled insects could crawl into a crack, the Mutilator was upon them, and had bolted every one.'

Banishment and disgrace followed for Mutilator fell from favour.

Calvin

Charles Dudley Warner in his book *My Summer in a Garden* wrote of his constancy to Calvin.

'I never had but one cat, and she was more of a friend and companion than a cat. When she departed this life I did not care to do as many men do when their partners die, take a second'.

Grisette, Mimy, Marmuse and Cafar

These cats and many more were immortalized by Francois Augustin, Paradis de Moncrif in his famous *Lettre Sur Les Chats*, first published in Paris in 1727. The names of these cats were many times recalled in song and verse by cat lovers the world over during the past 200 years. Moncrif himself set the balls rolling in his own 4 Scene TRAGEDY in which each cat played it's own Moncrif-stage-managed part and a dog called Cochon caused the great furore which ended in tragedy.

So 'what's in a name?' Much indeed, to those cat lovers of yesteryear.

8 The 'Poorly' Cat in a Bygone Age From Ass's Milk to Tinker's Mixture

'Save me, save me, you, who are a man!'

Besides being a distinguished man of letters Théophile Gautier was also a man of cats. His description of the last mortal hours of one of his beloved cats, so beautifully translated from the French by Mrs Cashel Hoey, is a moving panegyric.

'For hours together he lay stretched upon my knee like the shadow of a sphinx; I felt his spine under my finger-tips like the beads of a rosary, and he tried to respond to my caresses by a feeble purr that resembled a death-rattle. On the day of his death he was lying on his side panting, and suddenly, with a supreme effort, he rose and came to me. His large eyes were opened wide, and he gazed at me with a look of intense supplication a look that seemed to say, "Save me, save me, you, who are a man!" Then he uttered a lamentable cry of anguish'.

Théophile Gautier's heart bled and he instantly sent for the best doctor that was available. The doctor felt the cat's pulse, and sounded his lungs, and prescribed, as was his custom in all such emergencies, ass's milk. The cat died. Man could not save because man had no remedies. No more could man save himself, for two hundred years ago modern drugs were unknown and ass's milk was endowed with high curative properties for man and beast alike.

It was intended to be taken as an elixir of life, while, paradoxically, more often it was indeed a potion of death. The last quaff of earthly nourishment to kings and heroes of bygone days, was often, just ass's milk. When Louis XIV was on his deathbed, his leg half eaten away with gangrene, his physician, known as 'Fagon, the killer of princes' again boldly sent out his scout to fetch some ass's milk, but, meantime the King had passed away.

Very little better than ass's milk was on the pharmacopoeia for the treatment of disease in cats until about the middle of the nineteenth century, when it was first mooted that cats might be important and valuable, and that a little research in the use of other remedies would be perhaps helpful. Widespread epidemics of infectious diseases had recurred for many centuries. In 1796 the worst plague ever recorded wiped out every cat living in the stricken area, and cat lovers were alarmed. However, no serious thoughts were given to disease in the cat until Harrison Weir promoted them to high-class cats. Then it became necessary for humans to try and learn the art of alleviating pain and suffering in their pets. Now Harrison Weir enlisted the aid of prominent veterinary surgeons, setting out the symptoms and prognosis of disease and appealing for help. The symptoms presented for investigation are symptoms which we associate with feline enteritis and cat flu today. These diseases were then alternately classed as distemper and catarrhal fever.

They were then incurable. The symptoms described by Harrison Weir were:

'Intense fever, prostration, vomiting, diarrhoea, sneezing, cough, and profuse discharge from the nose and eyes. Sometimes the parotid glands were swollen as in mumps in humans'.

It would be difficult to isolate any one symptom, for every part of the body was infected. To attempt any form

of serious treatment with the means at their disposal proved to be a mammoth task. Most of the remedies tried were homœopathic in origin but strong beef tea, port wine and castor oil were much in use. For distemper, or fevers or catarrh there were many preparations tried.
Harrison Weir's prescription was:

> Basilicon, 1 oz.
> Flowers of sulphur ½ oz.
> Oil of juniper, 3 drams. Mix for ointment.
> Then give sulphide of mercury, 3 grains, two or three times on alternate nights.

As an aperient, Harrison Weir recommended a cat owner to:

> Get a chemist to rub down a medium-size croton bean with about 40 grains of sugar of milk, and divide into four powders. One of these powders usually sufficed.

For mange (or any skin diseases):

> In the early stages of mange, flowers of sulphur mixed in vaseline, and rubbed in the coat, is efficacious, giving sulphur in the milk, the water, and on the food of the patient; also give vegetable diet.
> Another remedy: give a teaspoonful of castor oil; next day give raw meat, dusted with flowers of sulphur.

For worms:

> Santonine, in a teaspoonful of castor oil.

Defeatism must have been a realism in the nineteenth century for in many cat books the methods of extermination of kittens and diseased cats was often given priority over the prolonging of life.

This was most probably because cat owners felt frustrated and helpless, for they knew that the remedies offered were of little value.

Miss Wilmslow, from whose writings I have derived much valuable information, and to whom I have referred

on so many occasions in this book, speaks of her method
of kitten annihilation, but the blows are considerably
softened by her gentle reasoning:

'In the case of unwanted kittens, I usually let the mother
keep one, and select a male for this purpose. The others I
immediately do up in a soft old rag, with a piece of brick
or stone, and deposit them in a pail of warm (not hot)
water. By following this method, and taking them soon
after they are ushered into this mortal world, a family of
small kittens can be carried into non-existence with no
knowledge of the transition on their own part'.

Many of her remedies are very similar to those used by
Harrison Weir; though in different continents, their ways
nearly crossed, and certainly at the time of her writing
Harrison Weir was still very much alive. Miss Wilmslow
too was very strong on homœopathic remedies, and found
many uses for aconite and belladonna. She, too, recommended santonine for worms, giving detailed information
as to its administration:

'The best possible remedy for worms is santonine, taken
in the form of one grain powders, three times a day on an
empty stomach, which is at least one hour before eating.
The latter precaution is very important, because the
worms, when the stomach is empty, seize upon and eat
the santonine, which is to them a deadly poison'.

For distemper or any of the serious infectious diseases,
Helen Wilmslow gives very scant advice, except to say
that it is wiser, perhaps to end the cat's misery before the
last terrible stages arrive.

'The most humane way to kill a cat is to chloroform it.
Put the cat in a small high box, or, better still, into a tin
wash-boiler, closely covered, in which you have first
placed a good-sized sponge wet with chloroform. In a few
moments the cat will become insensible, but do not take
her out of the box for at least thirty minutes, and then put
her in a pail of water head downward for another half
hour'.

At least if Miss Wilmslow could not cure a cat she could kill it!

Fleas seem to have worried many smart cats of yesteryear more than they do today. One lady who owned some of the best cats in U.S.A. made public her ways of 'assault and battery' when fleas became troublesome to some of her pets.

'She had ready a square of cotton batting and a square of cotton cloth; placing the cat in the centre of the batting, which had been laid over the cloth, she rubs strong spirit of camphor quickly into the fur and then gathers the corners of the batting and cloth tightly around the neck of the animal. She has a fine comb ready and a dish of hot water, for the pests, who detest the camphor, will run to the head of the cat, and must be combed out and plunged into the scalding water. Hundreds of them, however, will jump from the cat and lodge in the cotton batting, where their scaly feet stick in the cotton so they cannot get away. When the fleas cease to run out of the head of the cat, she judges that they have deserted the cat.'

With the establishment of pedigree cats the new breed of cat lovers were grateful for the first up-to-the-minute handbook published on cat management. Frances Simpson was the first writer to give cat lovers what they wanted; this was a simple down-to-earth treatise written in the language of the layman. In her first impressive book, *The Book of the Cat*, she did not attempt to elaborate on treatments but employed a veterinary surgeon to write a dissertation of a highly informative and scientific nature, which in those days must have been unique. But a quarter of a century later when her handbook was produced, she had had an accumulation of knowledge gleaned from wide experience in all aspects of cat behaviour, and consequently the book was a great success and many cat lovers became cat fanciers through the medium of its pages. Today of course her clinical methods would be frowned on, but her singlemindedness of purpose and her great love of cats have elevated her 'little yellow book' from being, not merely a collection of quotations and vignettes, but a classic any cat lover would want to grapple to his heart.

The pharmacopoeia published by Frances Simpson was strongly influenced by her great confidence in two veterinary chemists known by the names of Tinker and Salvo. In her opinion most of the illnesses of cats could be successfully treated by one or other of the capsules or potions which emanated from the famous specialists from Manchester. In addition to the orthodox treatments, which presumably were tried for the serious complaints there was going the rounds:

TINKER'S 'KIT-KAT' MIXTURE
SOOTHING, ANTISEPTIC, HEALING
PREVENTS AND CURES
DISTEMPER, SNUFFLES, FITS AND FEVERS

———————

WORM REPELLANT, BLOOD PURIFIER
AND RESTORATIVE TONIC

———————

Under this well-known advertisement which appeared in all cat papers of the day was a recommendation from Miss Frances Simpson:

'I have no hesitation in recommending Tinker's Mixture as a safe and sure remedy. I have tested it several times, and consider that all fanciers should keep it by them in case of need. It is a very good antiseptic stomach medicine, whilst for cats dull and listless, or which refuse their food, it is a wonderful restorative tonic'.

and another tribute from the same pen:

'I consider Tinker's Mixture a boon and a blessing to cat fanciers, and no one who values his pet should be without a bottle of this magic medicine. I know I recently warded off a serious attack by an immediate dosing, and before and after all shows I intend to resort to this effective concoction; whatever it is, it is absolutely safe'.

Yes, whatever it was the 'concoction' was a winner. What a pity Tinker took the secret of it to his grave!

As so many of our pedigree cats of today are direct descendants of the Fancy Cats of the Frances Simpson era it must be interesting for us to understand how their forbears lived and very often how they died. Even amongst the most carefully tended the mortality was high, and, with few exceptions, cats never reached the life-span of today. It is known that the Cat Fancy in those days was represented almost entirely by the wealthy upper classes, and they could afford to make good the losses; otherwise many of the less popular breeds might have disappeared.

Frances Simpson gave breeders of her day many things to think about, and gave breeders of today many things to smile about. It must be understood that she was speaking almost entirely 'ex cathedra' as the greatest cat fancier of the day when she made many of her pronouncements.

From Frances Simpson's *Little Yellow Book*

About Change of Air

There is no doubt that as a pick-me-up for delicate kittens the sea air is much to be recommended. It is quite wonderful to see the transformation in these little mites after a few days of sunshine by the sea. Their eyes become clear and bright and their appetites require something more than air and light to satisfy them.

On Diet

Oatmeal is such a splendid food for our pussies, but I find that few are partial to it. A little liver mixed in the meal sometimes makes it palatable.

Hovis bread (brown) with boiling milk poured over it is acceptable to most cats. Macaroni, well boiled and mixed with gravy is a capital food for cats and kittens. Fish, mixed with rice and boiled milk is relished by all pussies. A fowl's head, with the feathers on it, is said to be an excellent thing for cats. Sometimes when the appetite has quite failed, the sight of this delicacy will tempt pussy to start eating again. The same, if a sparrow can be trapped or shot, and given freshly killed.

Have you ever tried boiling sheep's heads until all the meat falls away from the bone, and then mixing it with some of its own gravy? It makes a delicious dish for pussy, and not an expensive one. I use rabbit's heads in the same way, and add some Freeman's scientific food with the meat to make it go farther.

It is a curious thing that all cats love asparagus, and it will tempt a cat who has lost his appetite. Some cats like beetroot and cheese is a delight to others. All can be recommended. I am not an advocate of tinned foods.

Distemper

When distemper attacks our poor pussies, there is really nothing to be done but to try to keep up their strength, as this disease often produces intense debility. Give frequent small doses of strong beef tea, into which one grain of quinine has been added. Also give small quantities of port wine. Brandy may be given as a last resource to arouse sinking vitality.

Fits

Fits are rather common amongst highly-bred cats, especially when teething. The following course is most effective: plunge the cat in a bath of water right up to its neck. Place a rag soaked in cold water on the head and bathe the face. By these means a cat will quickly recover.

Weak Chests

I do not like to see a cat, who, so to speak, mews without making any audible sound. This betokens a weakness. For this I would not advise lights. Instead a little chlorate of potash.

Lassitude

It is not a good sign to see a cat constantly sleeping in the daytime especially if we have every good reason to believe that puss had enjoyed a good night's rest. In such cases, give half a Carter's Little Liver pill, and you will find that your pet will be brighter and better.

Snuffles

A very tiresome complaint, and is nearly impossible to cure. I heard of one puss who was considered to be a chronic sufferer, and after a sojourn at the seaside she had not a snuffle left.

Eczema

Mix about two tablespoonfuls of colza oil with one of paraffin, with sufficient flour of sulphur to thicken the liquid. Mix well up. Divide the fur and rub well in with the fingers.

Fleas

For fleas I recommend Mr Tinker's powder. I hear that it acts like magic, and the pair of insect bellows supplied with it are a splendid invention which should be in the possession of all cat fanciers.

Worms

Several fanciers are under the delusion that castor oil is a universal cure for all ills, and they dose their cats accordingly. I have known this nasty stuff given for worms. Believe me, the worms thrive the more on it. and the result is upsetting poor pussie and causing her great discomfort.

If delicate kittens are dosed it sometimes finishes them off. It is just a matter whether the worms or the creatures are the stronger.

I recommend Freeman's capsules or Tinker's mixture in capsules.

Champion of Champions;
Roseway Cinderella.
Owner Mrs A. Peck

Spotlight Ricky Dicky.
Bred by Mrs P. Warner.
Owner Mrs Holt

Photo: Derek Davis Kent

Miss K. Yorke, Chairman of
the Governing Council, with
Champion Roseway
Cinderella, at Yorkshire
County Show at Harrogate,
when Cinderella won Best
Siamese In Show (1962)

Photo: Midland Press Agency

Miss Turner with Foreign Whites,
which she bred and owns

Hassan Jam Tart (Butterfly Rex)
breed; owned and bred by Mrs M
Shrouder

Photo: Raymond Garnett,

Champion Orlamonde de Khlaramour. Owner Mrs E. Fisher New Breed Bir
Bred in France

On 'Toms'

Don't forget to keep your Tom cats well supplied with grass, for having no amount of exercise they require it. Don't overwork him and avoid inbreeding. Stud cats require more meat and stimulating food than others, and a day should not pass without his having a plateful of meat, raw, if possible.

On Neuters

For reasons that are easily understood it is necessary, if you wish to have a house pet of unimpeachable manners, to have your cat doctored when he arrives at the years of discretion, or in this case I might say indiscretion! I consider between five and six months the best age for a cat to be gelded. In all cases a cat should be kept on a low plain diet for two or three days before being neutered, and it is more humane to pay for the cost of an anaesthetic. I have been told on authority that if a female cat has to be made neuter she ought to be allowed to have one litter before the operation is performed.

Miscellaneous

A very sure sign of a cat being out of sorts is when ears and nose are hot. Give an extra amount of green food or grass, and perhaps a little gentle aperient of some sort would not be amiss. I like to feel a damp, cold nose on a cat as well as a dog.

Remember that it is not the quantity of food that a cat takes that benefits it. The secret of its health and well-being is in the quantity it digests.

If you suspect an internal inflammation never give milk. I can testify from personal experience of the excellent preparations obtained from Tinker's, and Tinker's Magic Mixture, made up in capsules, should be in the possession of every fancier.

D

9 Neuters

Love of animals has always been traditional to the English way of Life. We were a nation of animal lovers in 1888, no less sincere than we are today. One in every four in the Victorian family kept a pet of one kind or another. Attempts had been made to domesticate all kinds of animals, but dogs won the first success. Next came cats and many families kept both dogs and cats. It was when the neutering of cats became common practice that they gained their first real popularity. The ordinary person felt that the keeping of entire cats presented too many complications, and when it was understood that cats could be so easily deprived of some of the most irksome of their natural functions, and could be adapted to man's requirements they took cats to their hearts, delighting in the new-style companion.

The fashionable Victorian cat was the Persian, and the fashionable Persian was, in most cases, a neuter. It was certain that no lady in high society would tolerate a male cat in her drawing-room, nor would she be embarrassed by the disturbances to routine of the constant arrival of kittens. So the new 'Breed' was not a Blue Persian or a Chinchilla, it was simply a neuter. This beautiful creature, with its exquisite flowing coat of softest texture, its wide-open and friendly eyes, its charm focussed on the person of its choice, proved itself to be fit companion for the finest lady in the land.

The popularizing of neuters, or geldings, as they were

then called, did more for the new Cat Fancy than any other one thing. Frances Simpson was so impressed with the improved sale of kittens, through describing them as neuters or 'household pet pussies' that she suggested that she might even make a speciality of keeping cats until they were old enough to be 'gelded' and then offering them for sale. It must be understood that the breeding of cats on a commercial basis was not yet fully developed, and Frances Simpson herself admitted to finding it difficult to obtain £3 for a prize winning Blue Persian. She also had many letters from new fanciers saying that many of the Short-Hair kittens fetched only 5s.

It was generally agreed that neutering had no ill effects; on the contrary, neutered cats retained their beauty and were seldom out of coat, and being stronger since neutering, they were more comfortable to live with. Their characters too became more mellow and they were more affectionate and docile than their undoctored kin. Personality changes too sometimes appeared. From being a shy little being, never seeking the limelight, a neutered cat may suddenly become a cheeky fellow, who will no longer sleep in the kitchen or the back porch, but pushes himself to the best chair in the drawing-room. And then, the change may be in the reverse order. To preserve the right equilibrium by avoiding any drastic changes, it was advised to neuter before development. In the case of females, the first fanciers thought it advisable to let the cat have a litter first, but 'spaying' was not done so generally as it is today.

Mrs Prescott Spofford, the American 19th century novelist, who so loved cats that she never omitted to introduce them to her writings. Talking about her six-toed neuter and the strange idiosyncrasies he had developed, said:

'Now Lucifer sucks his tail, alas, and alas! In vain have we peppered it, and pepper-sauced it, and dipped it in Worcestershire sauce and in aloes, and done it up in curl papers, and glued on it the fingers of old gloves. At last we gave it up in despair, and I took him and put his tail in his mouth, and told him to take his pleasure, and that is the reason, I suppose, that he attaches himself particularly to me.'

So popular had neuters become that almost all the well-known catteries kept a few neuters as house pets and as soon as cat shows were inaugurated, classes were included for neuters and there were often judged by weight. No matter what the breed, the bigger the better. Frances Simpson, who was the first twentieth century judge to bring reason to the judging of pedigree neuters wrote:

'Formerly neuters were judged by weight, and I remember some specimens exhibited at the Palace that really looked like pigs fatted for the market. It was in 1886 that the classification for neuters at the Crystal Palace show ran thus: "Gelded cats, not judged by weight, but for beauty of form, markings, etc." Happily therefore this state of things has been abolished, and though neuters should be big, massive cats, yet they should not, and need not, be lumps of inert fat and fur. It is true that a big show cat appeals to the non-exhibitor, and visitors to our shows are always greatly impressed with huge animals over-filling their all too small pens.'

Again, writing for Miss Simpson, Miss Cochrane, who herself kept many neuters, said:

'There are, without doubt, a great number of people who like to keep a cat, especially a Persian, for a pet pure and simple, one that can be the admiration of all, and of service in ridding the house of mice and rats. They will attain a greater size, and in nine cases out of ten retain all the pretty habits and antics of their kittenhood'.

'Zaida,' the well-known cat columnist in the early editions of *Fur and Feather*, wrote in 1901, urging the practice of neutering:

'For a perfect household pet the neuter cat holds its own. Too often the purchaser of a kitten starts breeding and multiplying a race of weedy, ill-kept animals, who do little credit to their owner. A cat with kittens is undoubtedly a charming sight; but a female cat is more or less a worry, and is, besides, only in coat for a very short time each year. Then a tom cat roams, fights and is often objectionable, but the stay-at-home cat is always a thing of beauty, never requires periods of seclusion, will mouse and rat with the best, and he is a credit to any establishment. In short, we would like to see more of them, not fewer, and a neuter class for every colour in the show. In many a household cats are now disliked through the ill-advised action of some member of the family in starting breeding with more zeal than knowledge, and without proper conveniences. If a lovely neuter, or even two or three, reigned supreme in their glory there would be an end to the trouble, to the groans of the other members of the family, to the "wasn't engaged to wait on cats" of the servants.'

Then followed a great period of popularity for neuters. Many famous cats were exhibited and many classes were put in the show schedules. The most famous neuter, whose picture has appeared in many old cat books, was Madame Portier's Blue Boy. One of his best show wins was at the Richmond Show when he presented himself in the Ring Class and was greatly admired 'for the dignified way he comported himself on a lead'. One of his greatest honours, his owner said, was on the occasion when he received a caress from the Princess of Wales. Many marvellous smokes won well in neuter classes, also some famous Chinchillas. Few of the early judges favoured Short-Hair neuters. Except for the odd Siamese, Miss Cartwright's 'Chute' and Lady Alexander's 'Blues', 'Brother Gamp' and 'Tom Gamp', all honours went to Persians.

Miss Simpson, then the most important all-round judge in the country, wrote of the judging of neuters:

'In judging neuters, I think it is a mistake to go too much by points. I consider that size should be the important factor, also coat and general effect. Of course, in close competition points would come into question; but I really think that a large, heavily coated neuter, whose colour was a trifle unsound, or whose markings or eyes were below par, should not be placed below a small, mean-looking cat, who, however, excelled in these points.'

Considering these lines, more than half a century later, one wonders if the 'small mean-looking cats' referred to in her judging notes were not just Short-Hairs after all!

Today's most important cats are neuters. The adored pets of the ladies of the lonely hearts are neuters. The cats that make the headlines in poetry and prose are invariably neuters and the breeding cat is a cat set apart for functional use only. Entire male cats are kept as stud cats and they live a cat's life only. But this kind of cat's life is not to be frowned on, for his owners follow the rules of the cat text-book which says:

'To keep a male cat in good condition he needs two good meals a day, and one of these should be of raw beef of at least a quarter of a lb. in weight. It is also recommended that during the mating season he should have a good third meal.'

So the life of the entire male is not to be scoffed at!

Neutering of cats today is done with great ease by expert veterinary surgeons. It should be done at about 5 to 6 months old, or whatever age recommended by the veterinary surgeon. The usual procedure is to take the kitten to the surgery, without having had any meal previously. He will be given a small anaesthetic and will be fully recovered in a matter of hours.

The neutering of a female cat is not quite so easy as that of the male, as the ovaries have to be removed and this is in every sense an operation which will require a little post-operative treatment. It is performed so expertly today that there are few casualties but, all the same, it is not good surgery to do it on a very young kitten. Sometimes the veterinary surgeon keeps the kitten overnight and when it returns next day to its home it is completely recovered.

The principal worry is to prevent the patient from removing the stitches. Today's spayed queen returns home with a plaster cast over her wounds and makes a great show of her operation scars. Many owners of spayed queens say they make the most delightful of all pets and that they are especially agreeable with children.

The geldings – the neuters – the 'household pet pussies' of the Simpson age are this generation's Top Cats.

Notes on present day Neuters

The Governing Council of the Cat Fancy granted the title of Premier in 1940 to cats winning the various Neuter classes offered at Championship Shows. The title of Premier is comparable with that of Champion and since its innovation much interest has been aroused and many truly lovely cats are shown in their respective classes. Some people feared that too many good kittens would be neutered thus depriving the Fancy of good prospective Studs and Brood Queens. This may be so, but on the other hand, neutered pets can be a great joy and certainly they usually live a carefree and happy life. Like Champions the title of Premier must be won three times under three different Judges and when they gain the full title they can enter in a special class 'Premier of Premiers' and compete against others of like rank.

To recall a few good cats who became Premiers after the title was approved:

Mrs H. Wilson's Long-Hair Cream, Pr. Priory Golden Glory
Miss Marshall's L.H. Blue, Pr. Trenton Verity
Mrs Calder's Chinchilla, Pr. Brocton's Merry Andrew
Miss Hardman's Short-Hair Tortoiseshell, Pr. Killinghall Oriel
Miss Bone's Abyssinian, Pr. Nigella Caliphe

Mrs Budd's British Blue, Pr. Nidderdale Bumble
Mrs Stuart's S.H. Silver Tabby, Pr. Culverden Gerard
Mrs Montgomery's Seal Point Siamese, Pr. Daybreak
Mrs Lambert's Seal Point Siamese, Pr. Firesprite Pedro

More recent Premiers are:

Mrs Trevor's L.H. Cream, Pr. Hendras Periander
Mr Shrimpton's L.H. Blue, Pr. Bartholomew of Pensford
Mrs Burgess' L.H. Blue Cream, Pr. Ronada Starlet
Mrs Beever's S.H. White, Pr. White Hawthorn
Mrs Lalandi Emery's Burmese, Pr. Ge Fay Isabella
Mrs Clark's Russian Blue, Pr. Petrovna Blue Peter
Mrs North's Blue Point Siamese, Pr. Whitehaugh Blue Nylon
Mrs M. Richard's Lilac Point Siamese, Pr. Praha Pavane
Mrs Williams' Seal Point Siamese, Pr. Hathor Hercules
Mrs Burrow's L.H. Blue, Pr. Bebe of Pensford
Mrs J. Richard's S.H. Cream, Pr. Bambi's Mischief
Mrs Grant Allen's S.H. Silver Tabby Pr. Elvaston Mist
Mrs Petre's Russian Blue Petrovna Blue Peter

Photo: Fetrographic

Champion Borrowdale Romeo (Orion's son). Bred by
Mrs E. Burrows, Owner Miss M. Graham

Champion Orion of Pensford.
Bred by Mrs J. Thompson
Owner Mrs E. Burrows

Photo: Petrographic

Champion Gaydene Amanda. Bred by Mrs McVady

10 *The American Cat Fancy*

The first important Cat Show to take place in U.S.A. was held at Madison Square Gardens, New York in 1895. Prior to this cat shows were quite common on a smaller scale, usually as adjuncts to poultry and pigeon shows. This first show, organized by an Englishman, James H. Hyde, was run on the same lines as the Crystal Palace Show in London, which he had recently attended. It might be said that this show was the one which initiated the Cat Fancy in America, for after this get-together of cat lovers a new era dawned for the cats of the U.S.A.

There were about 200 cats on exhibition, including some non-domestic cats: ocelots, wild cats and civets. One of the principal judges was a Dr Huidekoper, and it was said of him in jest that his student days were given up to visiting cat exhibitions in Paris, Edinburgh and London, where he had acquired more cat lore than scientific knowledge. Perhaps his promoting to top honours of a neutered Brown Tabby could be called into question, for such a cat could make no impact on the future generations. There were about a dozen English cats, and all won well here, having had their trial runs at Crystal Palace. White cats were the most popular, being headed by a well-known cat called Ajax, who died soon after the show.

After the second New York show, The American Cat Club was founded and Dr Huidekoper was inaugurated as first president. The objects, according to the first minutes written up were:

The American Club is organized for the purpose of investigating, ascertaining and keeping a record of the pedigrees of cats, and of instituting, maintaining, controlling and publishing a stud book or book of registry of such kind of domestic animals in the United States of America and Canada, and the purpose of promoting and holding exhibitions of such animals, and generally for the purpose of improving the breed thereof, and educating the public in its knowledge of the various breeds and varieties of cats.

But, in spite of its high ideals and excellent membership of the worthy the American Cat Club became comatose and faded out. It was immediately replaced by the Atlantic Cat Club, and this became one of the most powerful factors in the growth of the American Cat Fancy. The success of this club was due largely to the personality of its secretary, Dr Ottolengui who was a great organizer and a cat breeder of high standards. He kept a large cattery in which there were many English bred cats. His example influenced others and many catteries sprung up. The breeding of pedigree cats was found to be a lucrative as well as enjoyable hobby. Smokes and Silvers fetched very high prices, as they were then new breeds in the U.S.A.

Chicago was next on the scene, with the establishment of the Beresford Cat Club in 1899. This club was the most successful to date. Its president, Mrs Clinton Locke, was already a well-known cat breeder on both sides of the world. She was a member of many English cat clubs and had exhibited at many of the English shows; also she had imported good stock from England. She had in her time possessed every breed of cat even Siamese. She was Number One personality in the American cat world and the very great success and permanence of the Beresford Cat Club must be attributed to her zeal in every branch of cat activities. She was the wife of a clergyman and had succeeded in turning her kennels into a profitable undertaking; from her income so derived she was able to help many charities. One of her treasures was a bona fide cat mummy which was brought from Egypt, and which was verified by the Gizeh museum to be 4,000 years old. There was no doubt whatever that Mrs Locke was the fancier 'par excellence' of the newly established American Cat Fancy.

Apart from organizing many successful shows in which some really high-class cats were exhibited, the club did excellent work in every field of cat activity, having established a home for stray and homeless cats, and excellent boarding kennels, which at that time was a great innovation for the care and comfort of cats. The club was also incorporated under the state laws of Illinois. The Chicago Cat Club affiliated with the Pet Dog show and small dogs and cavies were exhibited at their first show. It was said that many of the best people in the United States were members of the Beresford Cat Club, and on the honorary list were such names as Agnes Repplier, Madame Ronner, Lady Marcus Beresford, Helen Wilmslow, and Louis Wain.

With the premier cat clubs well established the American Cat Fancy took permanent shape. In every state cat clubs came into existence and very soon they were more numerous than in England. Almost simultaneously with the Beresford Cat Club, cat clubs appeared in Detroit and far-away California. The Detroit fanciers made their ways to Chicago and New York shows, exhibiting English imported cats, and nearly always the honours went to Short-Hair Tabbies, which seemed to have found most favour; the odd Manx of good type occasionally was recognized. California immediately plumped for the Siamese, seeing in this exotic breed cats that would enjoy the warmth and sunshine of the Californian climate, and at one of the first shows these Siamese appeared in greater numbers than at any other American show at that time.

Soon the first inkling of a Cat Fancy was heard in Canada, and several well-bred English cats set things going at Toronto for the first cat show. Again there was a preponderance of Tabbies and a record was kept of a magnificent Brown Tabby who was imported from Ireland, a country little connected with pedigree cats. This short-legged bone-formation-conscious, well-marked male sired many 'Paddys' of high repute.

Only two judges operated at the first shows, and this situation did not help matter in the eyes of many newly-ordained cat fanciers, for these first-elect of judges did not really see eye to eye with each other with regard to standards. They were hampered too by lack of quality. Size was contended to be a factor in beauty, and was one of the greatest bogies with which a judge had to contend; American fanciers clung to an admiration of impressive physique even long after the arrival of pedigree cats and the certain pronouncements about difference in style made little impact. It was found to be extraordinarily difficult to convince fanciers that some cats should be small and dainty, whilst others are better cats if bigger and stronger, according to what breeds they represent. The presence of white hair in self-coloured cats, though tabu in England, and a certainty for disqualification at championship shows, was not frowned on. One American judge remarking about these faulty contestants wrote:

'Cats with white hair are much in favour here as with Continental fanciers; and, if so, there seems to be no reason for discouraging them, and we may as well make up our minds to the fact that in trying to force English ideas down the throats of the people of another country with too violent a hand, we may do a lasting injury to the Fancy at large.'

And so, with the approval of the early doyens of the American Fancy white hairs continued for many years to find favour. The long-haired exhibits were judged more or less as they appeared on the day of the show and this was not approved by many fanciers who found that their high-class cats were often out of coat and put down for this reason. But the reply to this was given by the same eminent judge:

'The average American exhibitor does not favour giving prizes to long-haired cats when out of coat, and the strength of the Fancy and its future popularity lies in presenting to the public the cats in their best dress, and this mostly is the logical way we can give out the principal prizes and appeal to the good sense of those who come to see them; for the general public, when not experts, can only judge from appearances.'

But the finer points of judging were soon resolved and gradually the teething troubles were over. The American Cat Lover became the American Cat Fancier! Over the years the American Cat Fancier and the English Cat Fancier sought no isolation from each other and a great and lasting affection grew up between our two great Cat Fancys.

During the period of the First World War, and after by reason of our sore distress, we lost contact a little with our fancier friends in U.S.A., and certainly the resuscitation of my own image of the American Cat Fancy occurred in 1938 when I found in my National Geographic Frederick B. Eddy's illuminating article on the pedigree cats of the American continent. This proved to my satisfaction that the pedigree cat was firmly established in the American way of life.

I quote from his article entitled: *The Panther on the Hearth*:

'Just as every agency for the care of dogs exist today, so the cat, though perhaps in lesser degree, is catered to. Veterinarians are paying much attention to puss than in former years. Serums and inoculations are at hand for the most deadly scourges of catdom. The canine kitchen that serve your dog will be glad to cater for your cat, and the beauty parlours that glorify the American dog will do a good job on your cat.

'Man and woman go abroad to obtain fine specimens of the various breeds, and pay sometimes hundreds of dollars for specimens which have outstanding records at the cat shows in England and on the Continent. In our country at present the most popular cat is the Long-Hair or Persian, and of this variety, the Blue Long-Hair, the most numerous at shows, seems to be holding its own. The Silver Tabby is deservedly popular and to my prejudiced way of thinking there are few animate creatures handsomer than a striking specimen of the Black Long-Hair. The Siamese is also coming into its own here as it has done in England. While our Siamese Cat Society shows seldom bench more than 50 specimens in England the Siamese Cat Club thinks nothing of caging 150–200 entries.'

Frederick Eddy, who was one time president of the Siamese Cat Society of America, paid a special tribute to the Siamese Cat of the nineteen-thirties.

'Striking in appearance, utterly unlike any other cat in colouring, this blue-eyed oriental consort of kings in his native Siam, is fast becoming a favourite among all classes of Americans'.

At that time he said that the Seal-Points were the most favoured, and that the Chocolate and Blue-Points were rare.

'The Blue-Point is not quite so striking as the Seal-Point, but it has a tonal beauty that reminds one of the Copenhagen china cats one sees in gift shops'.

Further in his long article on cats all the known breeds were mentioned and given standards for judging which were almost the same as for cats in Britain. This was to be expected as cats imported from Britain played such an important role in the foundation of the American Cat Fancy. The stud books issued by the various organizations identify British bred cats as the dynasty makers of the new era.

In principle the American Cat Fancy developed on similar lines to ours, but on account of the vastness of the American continent one controlling body was not practical; so, in the course of time, instead of having one Governing Council, five separate organizations were created to govern the cat world of the U.S.A. There is a slight difference in administration between them. Breed recognition is not absolutely identical. The organization of shows varies from one state to another, according to the controlling body's specification. In U.S.A. the pattern of shows is different to those held in Britain. Shows can be of either one, two or three day duration and, in some cases the cats can be removed when the closing time has arrived, and, of course, brought back on the following day for further exhibition judging. Kittens are usually judged first and they do not attend again.

The ornamentation of pens is permitted; in some shows it is only permitted to decorate the top of the pen. The judges have an enclosure where they view the cats undisturbed and it is usual for a fee to be paid to judges for their services. Veterinary inspection is essential before penning an exhibit and cats are very carefully scrutinized and turned away if there is any sign of skin disease, running eyes, ears or nose, and in most other matters the show is run on similar lines to ours.

Honours are handed out differently and are awarded on a points system. The number of entries at a show determine the number of points that can be won and a cat must have won ten points to be eligible for Championship status. These points can be made up by competition, that is open class winner against novice winner, colour and sex divisions and so on. Grand Champions are cats that have won 'Best Champion' under three judges and in the Grand Champion class one point is given for every three champions competing. At big shows, where there are five speciality judges it could be possible for a cat to become a Grand Champion at one show.

It is interesting to read that the various organizations can donate vast sums to charities from their show profits. Unfortunately, in Britain, the best that most show managers can hope for is that they will be able to break even. Perhaps one day a Golden Era will dawn in England for the pedigree cat!

11 The Governing Council of The Cat Fancy: Cat Clubs: Cat Shows

As soon as Cat Shows were inaugurated and a standard of points agreed, an interest in pedigree cats began. The new fanciers immediately set about giving permanence to their hobby by the establishment of cat clubs. The first important one to set its roots firmly in English soil was the National Cat Club. This was founded in 1893; but this was more than a cat club, it was a governing body, and for over twenty years it controlled registrations, kept a stud book and organized cat shows. The rival body to the National, The Cat Club, was founded by some of the most important people in the land, including the charming Lady Marcus Beresford, of whom I have written about so much in other chapters. This club was a governing body too, keeping its stud book and register, as did the National, and exhibitors who wished to show their cats in Cat Club shows had to register again with the Cat Club. This caused great confusion, and many tears were shed in an effort to attain sovereignty. The question of deciding Who was Who was never established, and after about five weary years of wrangling and bitterness, Lady Marcus, who had done so much for the welfare of cats, left the Cat Fancy and the Cat Club was disbanded, leaving the National Cat Club, holding most sway.

But the unsettled state of affairs amongst the leaders

112

did not put a stopper to progress, and soon many new clubs were established. The first specialist clubs which were inaugurated in the first years of the twentieth century, were the Siamese Cat Club, The Blue Persian Cat Society, The Manx Cat Club, The Black & White, The Silver & Smoke, The Orange Cream and Tortoise-shell, and The Short-Hair Cat Society. The first regional All-Breeds Clubs were the Scottish, founded in 1894, the Northern Counties in 1900, the Midland Counties in 1904 and the Southern Counties in 1905. Others which are now defunct, were Newbury, Richmond, Wilson's Cat Club.

Though clubs were flourishing the lack of leadership continued to cause friction, and in 1910, a move was made to establish unity. Representatives of the various clubs already mentioned assembled in London and agreed to amalgamate under one governing body. Shaping their constitution on almost similar lines to the Kennel Club, which was then handling the affairs of dog so satisfactorily, the Governing Council of the Cat Fancy was inaugurated. Amongst the important names associated with its chairmanship are the late Mr Russell Biggs, the late Sir Claud Alexander, the late Cyril Yates, and Miss Kit Wilson and Miss K. Yorke, the present chairman.

Then followed a great period of prosperity for the British Cat Fancy and the Governing Council assumed the role of leadership which was never disputed. From 1910 onwards there was a rapid growth in cat clubs and, except for the distractions caused by two world wars, the Fancy grew from strength to strength. Amongst the old-established Clubs, which came after 1910, were Croydon, founded in 1919, Siamese Cat Society of the British Empire in 1924, Yorkshire County in 1927. Quite a few clubs now affiliated were founded post-war, including Notts & Derby which has just celebrated its 21st birthday.

In 1953, the following clubs were already affiliated to the Governing Council of the Cat Fancy:

Abyssinian
Black & White
Blue Persian
Blue-Pointed Siamese Cat Club
Chinchilla, Silver & Smoke
Croydon
Edinburgh & East Scotland
Herts & Middlesex
Kensington Kitten & Neuter
Lancs & N. West
Midland Counties
National Cat Club
Notts & Derby
Red, Cream, Tortoiseshell, Tortoiseshell & White, Blue-Cream and Brown Tabby Socy
Russian Blue
Scottish Cat Club
Short-hair Cat Society
Siamese Cat Club
Siamese Cat Society of The British Empire
South Western Counties
Southern Counties
Southsea Cat Club
Yorkshire County

Ten years later the following clubs were added:

Burmese Cat Club
Chocolate Pointed Cat Club
Coventry & Leicester
The Isle of Wight
Northern Counties
Siamese Cat Association
Suffolk & Norfolk
Wessex Cat Club
West of England & South Wales

Again the list published in 1966 showed more additions:

Cheshire Area Cat Club
Preston Cat Club
Northern Siamese Cat Society
Lilac Pointed Cat Club
Lynx-Pointed Cat Club
Shadow-Point and Progressive Breeders Cat Club

Several clubs which started with great enthusiasm for one reason or another just petered out. The Hull & Lincs Cat Club, founded in 1961, served a keen community of cat lovers, yet for want of workers it had to be disbanded in 1964. This was a great loss to the Cat Fancy for the founder, Mrs K. Brough, was one of our most enthusiastic fanciers.

Cat Clubs are not the most harmonious of organizations and it does not follow that people brought together by their love of cats will automatically love each other. On the contrary, this kind of association does not always bring friendship, and, the Fancy, through petty jealousies, has lost many zealous workers.

The Secretary and Show manager are the dominant personalities in a cat club, for these are the real workers who give character to the setting. The work of a secretary is very arduous, especially when so many club members overlook the fact that her work is purely honorary. Many hours of her time and many shillings of her own money go voluntarily to the club, and sometimes committee and ordinary members are hard task masters. The office of a treasurer too is not to be overlooked, as accounts have to be kept and statements rendered.

A Show Manager's task is a very difficult one. With the great increase in the number of show goers, more time has to be given to expanding catering services. Pens have to be provided. Judges have to be assembled. Award cards and boards have to be set out and the show manager has to set the show in motion. All the receiving of money and the pay-out of money falls to the show manager; very fortunate indeed is the show manager who can make a profit on his show today. The actual presentation of the show rarely brings in a profit, so lucky is the show manager who finds on his committee, workers who organize raffles, jumble sales and tombolas, which help so considerably to balance his books.

The Governing Council has the last say in all matters of controversy or indecision. For fifty-five years, composed of delegates from the affiliated clubs, it has presided over the destiny of the British Cat Fancy. The main objects of the Council are to provide for the registration of cats and cat pedigrees, to classify cat breeds, to protect the welfare of the cat and cat breeders generally and to act as an arbiter in all matters affecting the feline world. A proposed new constitution is being shaped and delegates from all the affiliated clubs meet frequently at the Council Rooms in London to discuss its implications. The proposed new constitution, when agreed, will 'govern the affairs of the Cat World for possibly, ten to twenty-five years ahead'.

The Governing Council controls most effectively the running of shows. It does not itself run shows, but in 1960, under the direction of the late A. Towe, it held its Jubilee Show at Olympia. Registered cats cannot be shown in any show unless held under Governing Council rules, without special written permission, and all cat shows held in Britain, in which Governing Council approved judges operate, must be given approval. Before this is given the Council take note of the venue, the show promoters, and the show manager. The Governing Council, if it is assured of capable managing, writes to the show manager to say that the Council has given permission to hold an Exemption Show. The Council issues simple rules, insisting as well, that, wherever the show is advertised it must clearly state that it is being run under the Rules of The Governing Council of the Cat Fancy. A long folder, setting out many rules dealing with the registration breeding and classification of cats should accompany every schedule issued. The catalogue then must publish the Rules for the correct running of an Exemption Show.

Novices arriving at an Exemption Show cannot be excused transgressions if they have read the rules, which briefly are summarized below:

(1) Cats must be registered, and if newly acquired must have been transferred to the name of the exhibitor
(2) Cats must not be brought to the Hall on a lead but in a suitable basket
(3) Each cat should be provided with a clean white

blanket, drinking and feeding bowls, sanitary tray, and, of course, it must be wearing its disc on a white ribbon or elastic. The show manager provides the pen, with the number of the exhibit attached, also peat moss and drinking water. Food is not supplied

(4) Cats must be in good health and perfectly clean, with special attention being paid to the ears

It has now been made a rule that a period of two weeks should elapse between shows for any one cat. All cats have to pass the veterinary inspection and if there is any query it is well to get the advice of the show manager, who may ask you and your cat to leave the Hall.

Cats are judged absolutely on their own merits and anonymity is essential. At a time stated in the catalogue, which is usually at about 10 a.m., the show manager requests the exhibitors to leave the hall, and then the judges and stewards make their appearances.

Good judges are very important to the Cat Fancy, and are selected with great care. The newcomer to judging is first nominated by a specialist club, and must be a person of good character who has hitherto been identified with many Cat Fancy activities; club official, show manager, breeder of good cats, exhibitor at shows, or having had a long period of stewarding under many different judges. After a period of probation, in which kittens only are judged in open classes at championship shows, as well as miscellaneous classes, the person, if approved, is promoted to being a full judge of her speciality. Later, if she has experience of other breeds, she may be put on another judging list. Amongst the few remaining all-round judges are Miss Yorke, Miss Wilson and Mrs Thompson.

Various schemes have been tried to set a higher judging standard. In 1957 Miss Yorke inaugurated 'Classes For Judges', and these were exceedingly popular, and of great value to novice judges, as well as to those who were not familiar with all breeds. Several cats were used as models to illustrate good and bad points, and many well known judges gave to newcomers the benefit of their long experiences. Miss Yorke, herself one of the best of our all-round judges, emphasized many angles of judging that tended to be overlooked. She quoted from Council Rule 11, illustrating that:

'A cat which cannot be taken out of its pen must not be judged. An exhibitor is not allowed to take any of his exhibits out of the pen or to handle them during the judging. Transgression of this rule must result in disqualification of the exhibit'. So it is most important for exhibitors to understand that cats of unreliable temperament should not be shown.

At the show each judge is accompanied by a steward, who may be the judge's own selection, or allocated by the show manager. She is expected to identify herself by wearing a white coat and her badge of office. The steward should not accompany a judge if any exhibit of hers is entered in the Open Class.

Each cat is placed on a table and before the judging starts both judge and steward disinfect their hands in the bowls supplied. The judge then studies the good points of the exhibit, and, though the 'Point System' is not generally used today, the judge immediately knows which are the good points. Inwardly she has noted the bad points, which may not be too noticeable on first sight. In the case of an adult, whose first prize may mean the awarding of a Challenge Certificate, a good judge has to be very careful that the cat is a worthy winner. She studies his overall appearance, his type, his eye colour and set, his coat texture and colour, the length of his tail, and whether it is whipped or otherwise, his general condition, and she assesses his value in comparison to the other cats in his class. In the case of a kitten a little latitude may be allowed, as growing kittens vary a lot with each passing week, and in the case of Siamese, the points may not be fully developed and the true beauty of exhibits cannot be assessed. Judging on type is a very safe basis to work on, for once the exhibit is well grown, type varies little.

The Judge's Book has three columns where the awards are written, the table gets one, the Award Board the other and the third is fixed in the book, for the judge's use only, and in the space provided she writes her notes briefly on each exhibit. Brevity must be a valuable asset to a judge as the book provided is of such minute dimensions that one must curtail one's eulogies.

From the tiny place provided in the Judge's book she has to extricate her notes, which she sends to the organ of the Cat Fancy, *Fur and Feather*, to reproduce. Considering how unmanageable the names are that the printers are presented with, their subsequent presentation to the public is very good indeed. Recently, on account of the extremely high costs of printing the judges have been asked to restrict their notes to a description of open classes, and some miscellaneous ones. Club classes, which had formerly made up the biggest bulk of reading matter, are not now published in *Fur and Feather*.

Prize cards must not be affixed to the pen until after the time stated on the catalogue for admittance by the public, nor can any changes be made after the names of the winners are published on the Award Board. The Red Cards are the important ones, for they point out that a First Prize has been won. Challenge Certificates are printed on silver cardboard and are very impressive, but are not put on the pen until the judging has finished. Exhibitors are not permitted to remove their cats until after the time stated for the closing of the show.

No Challenge or Premier certificates are won at Exemption or Sanction Shows, but Best in Show, and Best in Breed trophies can be awarded. Rosettes may only be put in circulation at the discretion of the show manager, and only cat clubs are permitted to present them. Individuals are encouraged to give personal specials for their favourite breeds, and these are best if they are presented as outright wins. The prize money available for winning exhibits is not great, and £1 10s. for an open class winner is only presented at a big show like the National Cat Club Show.

The high-light of a show is the Best in Show judging. The entries for this must be open class winners only. The selected judges sit round a table and vote silently on the cat of their choice, which is still anonymous, wearing only its numbered tally. Sometimes a referee judge has to be called in, and it is a rule at Championship and Sanction shows that a referee judge must be available. The winners are then removed to Best in Show pens where visitors and exhibitors crowd in the aisle.

Payment of prize money is not permitted until the results are checked by the Registrar, and approved by the Governing Council. This is to ensure that no mistakes have been made in classification and that the descriptions of the exhibits tally exactly with the details in the possession of the Registrar.

Good wins at shows boost considerably the ego of a cat owner and the value of a cat can change overnight.

This cutting from the *Shields Gazette*, clearly illustrates that for all livestock, as well as for small animals, the difference between the values of show winners and their less fortunate brothers, is beyond reckoning.

The Poor Relation

Lindertis Eventful, half-brother of the Aberdeen-Angus bull Lindertis Evulse, sold at Perth yesterday for £63,000, was himself sold today. The price: £75 12s.

'Why Shows?' That is the answer.

Photo: Wally Talbot & Sons, Blackburn

Champion Snowwhite Gazelle. Owner/breeder Mrs J. A. Hogan

Champion Sweet Sultan,
Champion Sweet Cecily,
Kittens – Stella and Sweet
Tiffin. Owner/breeder
Miss M. Duff

12 The Recognized New Breeds

When a new breed has been recognized by the Governing Council of the Cat Fancy it immediately steps into line with all other registered cats and is given a breed number. This number identifies the particular breed for all time. Several suggestions have been put to the Council about re-shaping the pattern of numbering but the system started by the pioneer fanciers seems still to be working well, and there is no reason for altering it.

In the nineteen-twenties, when the Cat Fancy came to life again after World War I, the following was the breed list submitted to all members of the National Cat Club, the premier club of the day:

Long-Haired Cats	*Short-Haired Cats*
1. Black	15. Black
2. White	16. Blue
3. Blue	16a. Blue Foreign
4. Red or orange	17. Cream
5. Cream	18. Silver Tabby
6. Smoke	19. Red Tabby
7. Silver Tabby	20. Brown Tabby
8. Brown Tabby	21. Tortoiseshell
9. Red or Orange Tabby	22. Tortoiseshell & White
10. Chinchilla	23. Abyssinian
11. Tortoiseshell	24. Siamese
12. Tortoiseshell & White	25. Manx
13. Any Other Colour	26. Any Other Variety
14. White	

Forty years later, after many changes had taken place in the whole structure of the Cat Fancy, the List of approved breeds remains almost constant. Below is the Breed Number now issued by the Governing Council to all persons concerned with the breeding and showing of pedigree cats. Where additions were made the change was brought about by the addition of a letter, except for the change of Breed Number 13, which used to read Any Other Colour and is now the number given to Blue Creams, and, in the Short Hair variety, in addition to the new varieties with the old numbers and letters, there are 27, 28 and 29, added.

Breed Numbers 1966

Long-Haired Cats	New Additions
1. Black	
2. White	
2a. White (Orange Eyes)	2a
3. Blue	
4. Red Self	
5. Cream	
6. Smoke	
7. Silver Tabby	
8. Brown Tabby	
9. Red Tabby	
10. Chinchilla	
11. Tortoiseshell	
12. Tortoiseshell-and-White	
13. Blue Cream	13
13a. Any Other Colour	
13b. Colour Point	13b
14. White (Blue Eyes)	
14a. White (Orange Eyes)	14a
15. Black	
16. Blue British	
16a. Blue Russian	16a
17. Cream	

Short-Haired Cats	*New Additions*
18. Silver Tabby	
19. Red Tabby	
20. Brown Tabby	
21. Tortoiseshell	
22. Tortoiseshell-and-White	
23. Abyssinian	
23a. Red Abyssinian	23a
24. Seal-Pointed Siamese	
24a. Blue-Pointed Siamese	24a
24b. Chocolate-Pointed Siamese	24b
24c. Lilac-Pointed Siamese	24c
25. Manx	
26. Any Other Variety	
27. Burmese	27
27a. Blue Burmese	27a
28. Blue Cream	28
29. Chestnut Brown Foreign	29

The new numbers do not follow any sequence and are fitted in just as near as they can be to the number of their first known variety.

(A) 2a, is the number given to Long-Hair Whites with only the small difference of eye colour, which, according to the new standard should be Orange or Copper. It was about 1938 that the new definitions were given. The stepping up of Orange-eyes Whites to Championship status was well received, for though the two Whites were equally beautiful with regard to length of coat and beautiful lustre, the Blue-eyed Whites were definitely not such good breeders, and it was always understood that they were handicapped by deafness; the Orange-eyed Whites, however, were more predictable in their breeding habits, and certain other differences to their advantage were observed by breeders.

(B) 14a, referring to Short-Hairs with varying eye colour which were recognized about the same time. The pattern of their lives is very similar to their Long-Haired White relations.

(C) 13. This beautiful cat, with the intermingled pastel shades of Blue and Cream, giving a shot-silk impression, has the title of Blue Cream. These came into prominence about the late thirties, but they never became very common, because it was found difficult to get the softly intermingled coats so desired in the standards agreed by the specialist club.

(D) 13b. This beautiful post-war, English-fashioned cat, known as a Colour-Point, has been given as its Breed number 13b. It received recognition by the Governing Council of the Cat Fancy in 1955. Many well-known fanciers were responsible for the final evolution of a Long-Hair cat with the colour distribution and markings of a Siamese, and the type, structure and long hair of a Persian. Miss Collins of the Kala prefix, who lives at Worthing, bred Colour-Points experimentally with Siamese and Long Hair Blue, Black and Cream about 1949. One of the first known Colour points was of her breeding. Later Brian Stirling-Webb, with others, further developed the breed as it is known today. The Colour-Point was not unknown in America, for breeders had been trying out many experiments before the war, but they had not followed these through to completion.

A Colour-Point can be either Seal-Pointed, Blue-Pointed or Chocolate-Pointed, with the appropriate body colouring for the true Siamese, but the head should be broad and round, with short nose and face, and, like Siamese, the eyes should be blue. Any similarity in type to Siamese is undesirable.

(E) 16a. This number was given to the Russian Blue when it was officially recognized by the Governing Council in 1948. It was sometimes known as the Blue Russian or the Archangel Cat. This is a very attractive cat of foreign type but resembling the British Blue in colouring. Its admirers says that it is definitely associated with the

Palace Cats of Russia. The Standard of Points was revised in 1952, when its difference from the British Blue was emphasized, 'its body being long, lithe and sinuous, fine in bone, with a long, narrow skull and receding forehead'. Again in the description of the breed, it was stated that the primary feature and one that distinguished it from all other cats, blue or otherwise, is the coat, which is short, close and lustrous. Russian Blues have been exhibited from the very earliest days of the Fancy and have been described amongst the 'First Known Short-Hairs'. There had been great confusion about designation, and in show catalogues in 1921 they were sometimes described as Self Blue, foreign type. To illustrate the desire of the owners to keep the breed Russian, names such as Prince Igor, Prince Romanoff, Peter The Great, Nadia, Paddiwiski were found in the catalogues about that period.

(F) 23a. Red Abyssinians have appeared in litters for a number of years, and are quite distinct from the well-known older generation of Abyssinians, whose coat colour was ruddy brown ticked with black or dark brown. Mrs Dorothy Winsor gave me her impressions which I published in *Cats In Clover* and extracts are quoted here. Of her first Red she said:

'Her coat gradually changed to a deep ticked red which glowed like a flame – a colour so solid and lovely that I wanted not merely to breed from her, but to breed kittens of the same vivid colouring'.

Mrs Winsor, through the *Abyssinian Newsletter*, contacted several people who were interested and set about breeding from the few Reds then available. With the help of the Abyssinian Cat Club, and the great interest of both Miss Bone and Mrs Menezes, Red Abyssinians came into the official register. At one time grey Abyssinians were identified and were invariably listed in catalogues as Silver Abyssinian or Aluminiums.

(G) 24a. Though Blue-Pointed Siamese were known in the Cat Fancy for a number of years, the pioneer breeders did not think much of them, and Phil Wade actually tried to discourage their promotion. Yet she bred the first B.P. champion which was owned by Mrs Hindley. This cat was named Sayo of Bedale, winning its first Challenge Certificate at the Siamese Show of 1937, its second Challenge at Croydon in 1937, and its final at the National in the same year. The second well-known Champion was Miss Busteed's female, Champion Grisnez.

In 1947 the Blue-Pointed Cat Society was affiliated to the Governing Council and an alteration to the standard of points was made. The body colour which was first described as pale cream was then altered to read 'glacial white'.

With these important efforts to improve the Blue-Pointed cats the name of Major and Mrs Rendall must be forever associated. Under their patronage the Blue-Pointed Cat Club became a great force for good in the Siamese world. Attempts were made to introduce the 'Points System' of judging wholly, but this was not entirely satisfactory, for a cat with some very bad points could make up on its good ones, the result being that a First Prize winner, with a quota of high marks could still be freakish in some respects. This could have been overcome if they had introduced at the same time a system of 'Penalty marks' for bad faults. Mrs P. Lauder was another important pioneer breeder. Through her writings and contacts abroad, the name of Phyllis Lauder, must be forever synonymous with the breeding of high-class Blue-Pointed Siamese.

(H) 24b. All Chocolate-Pointed Siamese must be registered as belonging to Breed Number 24b. This type of Siamese was known in England from very early days, but never attained the popularity of the Seal-Pointed cats. Just before the 1939 war they had fallen completely out of favour. However, largely due to the endeavours of Miss Fitzwilliam and Miss V. Prentis in 1951, Chocolate-Points were given a breed number with a very attractive standard of points which called for – 'Milk Chocolate Points, with ears, mask, legs, paw and tail to be the same colour, and eyes to be bright vivid blue, and the coat should be ivory colour all over'. Cats of the Chocolate variety, which had achieved fame were Miss Prentis's Georgina and Mr Brian Stirling Webb's Homesdale Chocolate Soldier.

(I) 24c. Now we come to another variation in Siamese to be recognized. Lilac-Pointed Siamese, mostly referred to in U.S.A. as Frost-Pointed Siamese. These got their breed number in 1961. Though a very new breed they have jumped overnight into the first line of popularity and classes at shows now almost equal their step-sister Blues. The particular charm about them is their very delicate colouring, for the coat is pure white and retains this beautiful coat well into adult life; in this respect it overshadows the Blue-Pointed Siamese, the coats of which darken with age or assume a variation in fawn colour which is unattractive.

Many great fanciers were associated with the establishment of Lilac-Pointed cats: the late Mrs K. R. Williams founded the Lilac-Pointed Cat Club and was the secretary at the time of her death. It was recorded that she bred the first all-Lilac litter.

Mrs E. Fisher has had great interest in Lilacs and has produced for home and abroad many class Lilacs. Mrs Sayers is another important breeder who manages to combine complete charm of manner and youth with the serious business of cat breeding. Mrs Ashford from Kent, has exported some well-bred and remarkable Lilacs.

(J) 27. Brown Burmese. The first Burmese Cats in England were imported from America in 1949 by Mr and Mrs France of Derby, a male Casa Gatos Da Foong and an Unrelated female, American Ch. Laos Cheli Wat, by Mrs Blanche Warren of California. After six months in quarantine they made their first public appearance on television at Alexandra Palace and were put on exhibition the next day at the Croydon Cat Club Championship Show held at the Lime Grove baths, Hammersmith on November 10th, 1949, where they attracted much interest.

Although Burmese did not receive official recognition by the Governing Council of the Cat Fancy until three generations had been bred true to colour according to G.C. Rules, they were an established breed in America in the thirties, having been brought from India by Dr Thompson of San Francisco. Mrs France imported a second unrelated female, 'Chindwins Minou Twm' in 1950 and the Brown Burmese were soon established here and having produced three generations true to colour were given the breed number 27 by the G.C.C.F. By 1952 the first Championship classes were put on at the Croydon Cat Club Show held on November 13th of that year and Dr Attwell's female Chinki Yong Shwegalay, bred by Mrs France, won the first CH. certificate in a class of one male and five females. This cat had also produced the third generation of Brown Burmese in this country.

A second Brown male was imported in 1952, Casa Gatos Dar-Kee. The breed continued to prosper and by 1955 all the Burmese Cats had been taken over from Mrs France by Mr and Mrs Watson also of Derby, who have done much to further improve and popularise the breed. They formed the Burmese Cat Club in 1955, which is affiliated to the G.C., and is represented by a Delegate. The Club has a specialist Judge's list and issues an excellent News Sheet. Mr and Mrs Watson have since imported two more Brown Burmese males. One, an especially elegant cat, is Ch. Darsham Khudiram.

(K)27a. In 1955 a Blue kitten appeared in a litter bred by Mrs Watson later called Sealcoat Blue Surprise. Gradually the Blue strain was built up and in 1960 three generations of Blues having been produced the Governing Council gave the breed a subsidiary number of 27a. Separate classes for the two colours were put on at the Governing Council Cat Fancy Show held at Olympia on September 24th, 1960. Miss Dunn's male, Bulrushes Blue John and

Lacey giving a lesson on
nail sharpening

Photo: Dr Brian Eustace

International Champion
Hillcross Tawny.
Breeder Mrs E. Tome
Owner Mme Heyer

Photo: Serafino,

Ice Cream Puff, Persian Creme. Owner Mme Heyer

Persian Blanc.
Owner Mme Heyer

Photo: Serafino, Paris

Mrs Wallington's female, Arboreal Blue Pandora won their respective classes.

The standard of Points for these cats is similar to the American version, but the Blues are still rare in the U.S. Eye colour for the brown Burmese should be Chartreuse Yellow and those of Blue Burmese can sometimes be described as Agate Yellow flecked with brown or a lovely clear colour which I can only describe as golden turquoise. The Brown Cats have soft, silky, fine textured coats with a lovely sheen, white hairs or patches lose points for Show Cats, the Blues have rather thicker coats and the fur is not always quite so fine but their feet, which should be small and oval for all, are of a beautiful silvery tone. They should all have long tails, a kink is only permissible if at extreme tip. Females of both colours are usually rather small and dainty, males are bigger, well grown and elegant.

Miss K. MacPherson has established a first-class Burmese Cattery in the North of England, and even when our Northern climate is at its worst, the cats live outdoor without any artificial heating. Their houses are draught-proof and they have very warm bedding, and they usually sleep two in a bed. Their diet is rich country fare. Burmese cats have been exported to Europe, Ceylon, Australia and New Zealand.

(L) 28. The Blue Cream Short Hair. These cats are very difficult to breed to standards and are very rare. Their development follows the same lines as its Long Hair counterpart.

(M) 29. The Chestnut Brown Foreign is an English manufactured breed, and was recognized as a separate breed in 1960. The late Miss E. von Ullman, Mrs Fisher, Mrs Monro Smith and Mrs Hargreaves all worked together, pooling their knowledge and exchanging views on the new wonder cat that they had all helped to create. A mating between a black cat and a Chocolate-Pointed Siamese resulted in a self-coloured chocolate cat. Mrs Hargreaves, who had also been experimenting with Seal-

E

Pointed and Russian Blues also produced hybrids which were used in the establishing of the breed. The Chestnut Brown Foreign is a brown all-over cat, with a short, glossy coat and green eyes. It is of distinctly foreign type, with slim legs and dainty paws.

Many of the new breeds discussed in another chapter have now been recognized. Fanciers, whose interests lie in developing these breeds, will start 1967 with a feeling of achievement. There have been some changes in standard requirements for Lilac-Points and Russian Blues, Lilacs with regard to colour only but Russians in other respects as well. These are referred to later.

Breed No. 30. Spotted Cats

These must follow the general lines applicable to British cats, and any similarity to foreign type is a fault. As the name implies 'Spots', which can be either round, oblong or rosette-shaped, must be the distinguishing features, and they must also be in harmony with the eye colour and coat colour.

Breed No. 31. Bi-Coloured Cats

Like the 'Spotted' cats, these must be British in type, but are not altogether a new breed, as Bi-Coloureds, together with their close relatives the Tri-Coloureds, had breed numbers almost from the inception of the Cat Fancy. It is not quite understood when, and how, they lost their popularity. Bi-Coloureds should have the markings associated with Dutch rabbits. The self-colours of Black, Blue, Orange, and Cream should be combined with White, with the self colours starting immediately behind the shoulders, following a certain pattern in the new standard of points. Eye colour should be Copper, Orange or Amber.

Breed No. 12(a). Long-Hair Bi-Coloureds

This almost unknown breed should follow the same standards of colour applicable to Short Hairs.

Breed No. 13(c). Birmans

These remarkable cats are classed as Long-Hairs, and
have provisionally been given the same standards as those
applicable to Birmans in France, from which country they
have been imported into England by Mrs E. Fisher and
Mrs Richards. These cats have Siamese points, both Seal-
Point and Blue-Point. Only Blue in eye colour is recognized.
Their most distinguishing features are their white-gloved
paws, which really brand them as the Temple Cats of
Burma. They are not to be confused with the Long-Hair
Colour-Point, an entirely man-devised breed, referred to
in another chapter.

Many early cat historians claim that Siamese must
surely have descended from these two-tone cats. They were
certainly the first-known cats to have the Siamese-type
markings, and their identification as the Temple Cats of
ancient Burma few would dispute.

These Birman cats were recognized as a breed in France
in 1925. From Mrs Fisher's notes in *Cat World* I quote:

'These cats are not only beautiful, they are gentle,
sweet tempered, and very loving, very intelligent, and
have only a small soft voice. They walk with a majestic
tiger-like gait, have beautiful blue eyes, and a flowing coat
with a bushy tail. The points resemble the Siamese in
colouring, and, of course, their characteristics are their
four white feet. There are Seal and Blue Birmans. Their
prefix is "Paranjoti," meaning, Beautiful Ones.'

Breeds Nos. 32. Tabby-Point Siamese
*   32(a). Red-Point Siamese*
*   32(b). Tortie-Point Siamese*
*   32(c). Any other dilution Siamese*

These four new varieties are all Siamese in type. They
have been carefully and selectively bred through the
required three or four generations. Many names were
suggested, and Lynx and Shadow-Point, were discarded
for the quite ordinary name of Tabby-Point. The Tabby-

Point is the most popular of the new varieties, having appeared many times under Breed No. 26 (Any other variety). The body colour should be pale and free from markings. There should be no stripes on the ears, but the clear thumb mark should be visible. The mask should have clear stripes round the nose and eyes, and the legs should have varied broken stripes, with solid markings on the backs of legs. Other points are under consideration.

Mrs D. Clarke, judging at the Siamese Cat Club Championship Show in September, 1966, awarded the first Challenge Certificates to two of the new breeds. The Tabby-Point winner was Mrs Warner's Spotlight Penny-linx, 'a most attractive queen of excellent type', having 'well-marked mask and very distinct thumb marks on ears'. This cat made history for Mrs Warner, for not only did it win the first Challenge Certificate for the new breed, but it went on to win Best in Show, over all the other varieties of Siamese.

The Tortie-Point, owned by Mrs Von Hoensbroech, won the first Challenge Certificate for Tortie-Points, again making a very important step forward for another new breed. The 'marked blaze', stamping the cat as a Tortie Point, was accompanied by many other good Siamese points.

Red-Points have been slow in gaining recognition, and they are a very beautiful breed. They have been known for many years, Mrs K. R. Williams having written about them in her first published book on Siamese cats in 1950. They are much admired in the U.S.A., having developed on much the same lines as they have done in this country. With this breed the points must be unmistakably Red, the principal fault is a paleness and lack of lustre in the mask.

There are many other dilutions now recognized, and these are catered for in Breed No. 32(c). These varieties cannot yet be awarded a Challenge Certificate.

The new breeds have one essential in common, they must be Siamese in type, having tail, body length, eye colour and oriental set, right up to the required standards.

There has been a new look at the Lilac-Point standards. Body colour, formerly described as being Frosty White, shading, if any, to colour of the points. The body colour should now be described as 'Off-White-Magnolia' a new descriptive adjective applied to our pedigree cats. Points are now more precisely described as of pinkish grey, and nose leather and pads should be classified as to the colour of 'Faded Lilac'. Colour blindness would be a bad fault in a judge of Lilacs; luckily this is a male aberration.

Breed No. 16a. Blue Russian Cat

This very handsome breed, with such gentle characteristics, has at last got a good standard of points, which is already accepted as a great improvement. Formerly described as Russian Blues, it is now more correct to refer to them as Blue Russians. Medium Blue is approved in preference to the vagueness of Medium to Dark, hitherto written in the standards. There is a difference too, in the coat, and the new standards emphasize that the texture and appearance of the coat is 'the truest criterion' of the Blue Russians. The principal faults are, white or tabby markings, cobbiness or heaviness in build, squareness of the muzzle, and yellow in the eyes.

Today's new Breed List, contains 47 numbers. In some cases the breed is the old one, with differences in colour, and only classification is different, as in Long Hair Whites, Short Hair Whites, Siamese, Burmese, and Abyssinians. A show manager of a Championship Show must therefore put on open classes for every breed, sometimes dividing them into male and female. This is a great trial to the show organizers, as, with the rare breeds there may be only one in the class, and prize money would have to be paid. All adult cats that measure up to the official standards are eligible for Challenge Certificates, and even though the classes may be small, if they are separated into male and female, Challenge Certificates may be given for each. At a meeting of the Governing Council of The Cat Fancy held in 1935 the rule was passed that:

'When the number of exhibits in the two open classes is below seven, only one certificate should be given. If, however, the winner of the opposite sex be of very high quality the judge may be empowered to give the second championship, subject to the approval of another judge.'

What the exhibitors do not generally know is that show managers will willingly split classes, if he or she will guarantee one or both classes. 'Guarantee' means help with the prize money. All the classes which are not likely to be well filled could be helped by a sponsor, who is willing to pay the prize money if there are not enough entries to balance the books. In some areas, especially in the North, the Cat Fancy is in dire need of generous friends.

It is obligatory for Championship Shows to include Open classes for registered neuters. The winners of these classes are awarded Premier Certificates, if they measure up to the standards. Classification for these is as follows:

Any Colour Self Long-Hair
Any Other Colour Long-Hair
Any Variety British
Any Variety Foreign (ex Siamese)
Seal-Point Siamese
Any Other Colour Siamese

The same rules apply to the showing of neuters as to entire cats, but they cannot be entered in competition against each other. Neuters against neuters only.

The unrecognized breeds, if they are registered, must be entered in classes for *Any Other Colour* or *Any Other Variety*, for they must be given a place in which to show themselves.

Additions to Breed Numbers 1966 on Page 185

Long Hairs
12a. Bi-Coloureds
13c. Birmans

Short Hairs
  30. Spotted Cats
  31. Bi-Coloureds
  32. Tabby-Point Siamese
  32a. Red-Point Siamese
  32b. Tortie-Point Siamese
  32c. Any Other Dilution

And as the feline scene extends itself, so the heart of the cat lover extends itself too, for he must make room there for all the newcomers.

13 *Breeds of the Future,*
as yet Unrecognized

The Cat Fancy is a progressive organization. To a person of initiative and imagination it offers much to think about and much to do. Besides being just an ordinary cat lover, possessing only one neutered pet one can be a specialist breeder, and with the right kind of stock this can be rewarding both mentally and materially. However, the most exciting of all new ventures is to preside over the animal breeding machine and help in the creation of new breeds; if one is possessed of the 'green fingers' so coveted by the horticulturist, there is no limit to the extent to which one's energies can be directed. In this pattern of creation the cat fancier can outdo the human fancier whose experimental breeding has so far been limited to artificial insemination, and the augmentation of fertility.

The post-war years have brought many newcomers to the world of pedigree cats. Already some have overcome the hurdles placed in their paths and have finally entered the ranks of pedigree cats, wearing their official tag and launched to the cat world with the blessings of the Governing Council of the Cat Fancy. But many are yet undesignated, and for all show purposes these novices are lumped together in either of four classes. These classes must be made available to them in the schedule of all Championship All-Breed Shows, and actually at the large show like the National there were further sub-divisions.

These classes were:

(1) Any Other Colour Long-Hair Cat registered with the breed number 13

(2) Same for kitten

(3) Any Other Variety Short-Hair British registered breed 26 (National Cat Club Schedule only)

(4) Any Other Variety British Kitten, again registered with the breed No. 26 (National Cat Club Schedule only)

(5) Any Other Variety Foreign Cat registered number 26

(6) Any Other Variety Kitten registered number 26

All cats in these groups are registered, but they do not conform to any pattern, and, consequently, there are no standards for judging. These cats are first entered in the Supplementary Register, according to the rules for registration issued by the Governing Council of the Cat Fancy. This Supplementary Register contains:

(1) All cats of unknown parentage

(2) All cats which are the result of a cross between two breeds or between two cross breeds

(3) All cats not showing three generations of true breeding

The Governing Council will consider:

(1) That experimentally bred cats may be entered in the ordinary register when they show three generations of the same variety in their immediate ancestry

(2) That in the case of new varieties when three generations of true breeding are recorded, the Council may, at the request of the breeder, issue a breed number

It is also pointed out that a cat should be entered in the breed number to which she conforms no matter what her pedigree is. The Supplementary Register, used for all cats that do not conform to standards, is a very useful extension, making absolutely certain that the Register is complete having classes for every type or colour of cat.

Cats entered in Any Other Colour or Any Other Variety classes should not be placed in competition with other cats, nor are they ever eligible for Championships. Experimentally bred cats make up the bulk of the entries in these classes, though at recent shows all kinds are exhibited including Spotted Tabbies, which are coming back into favour and have applied for reinstatement in the numbered list approved by the Governing Council of the Cat Fancy. Accidentally bred cats very often appear, and sometimes these come to the fore in the award sheet, and by so doing set the balls rolling for interest in a new variety. As there are no standards available for judging, at each different show the judge's comments are often conflicting.

Experimental breeding should only be undertaken by a specialist who has expert knowledge of the science of genetics. It is true that many breeders can get by with little knowledge by adhering firmly to the old adage that 'like begets like', and if they stick rigidly to matching up of good with good, then good most likely will follow. This is successful enough with the established breeds, but to engage on a course of experiments with valuable livestock in a haphazard way is very wasteful and sometimes highly irresponsible. As the ultimate in experimental breeding is the production of the finished article, the cat that hopes to establish itself must wait for his denouement until three generations or more of true breeding can be vouched for. The experimental breeder who has got so far will have achieved something of which he can be justly proud.

The National Cat Club Show, referred to in *Our Cats* as 'The Greatest Show on Earth' held annually at Olympia, puts cat breeding in the right perspective. More than 1,000 cats appear for competition in the known breeds. There is also a section for Household Pets, and these are unregistered, and, if mature, must be neutered. The exhibition cats, in decorated pens, always draw great crowds. To an intending breeder a close study of these cats is well worth while. It is usual for the owners to be hovering in sight, and nothing delights them more than to talk about their special 'babes'. They can give very useful instructions about the management, and, if they have any attractive idiosyncrasies they make special play of it. Even before a breeder has thought of development of his newly discovered protegé an exhibition day at Olympia can give great encouragement and has many benefits. The new cat is seen and admired, his good points noted and emphasized, his new names debated on, and, in many cases, he has made such a hit that he is sure to be safely launched into the new world of pedigreed high-class cats.

For more than a decade now the Rex, the curly-coated cat, has aroused much interest amongst the selective breeders. It would appear that the arrival of the Rex cat is one of the most exciting things that has yet happened in the Cat Fancy. The Colour-Point and Any Other Variety Cat Club was the club mainly interested in developing this breed until a Rex Club was founded in 1964 and has now been affiliated to the Governing Council. Several well-known names are associated with the development of the Rex Cats: Mrs Madge Shrouder, Mrs Watts, Mrs Lauder, Mrs Ashford and Mr B. Stirling Webb have all bred and studied these wonder cats. Through their endeavours the Governing Council has now approved a provisional standard of points, and breeders welcome the addendum which says of the standard mooted that Rex cats should be of modified Foreign type.

Most breeders of Rex cats would agree that there is a lot of foreigner in the first curly cat that came to their notice. This cat was called Kallikunder, and was discovered in a farm in Cornwall over ten years ago. Though he himself had a short life he left behind him a curly son who mated his near relations thus keeping the ball rolling for the curly cats. A little while later another curly cat appeared in Devon and breeders were then able to establish that this cat belonged to the Gene 2 Rex, having not so profuse a coat as the Cornish cats, but more curly. Hairlessness was a factor in the Gene 2 Rex and Breeders described it as a fault which would have to be bred out. All colours of Rex cats are permitted.

Mrs Madge Shrouder has done more than anyone to popularize the breed, for, invariably when she goes about her business she is accompanied by her special pet, 'Du Bu Blackcurrant', a little Blackie, bred by Mrs Watts. 'Du Bu Blackcurrant' has justified her existence for she too, mated to 'Du Bu Fennic', has provided Mrs Shrouder with another little companion, this time a little boy friend called 'Hassan Jam Tart'. Altogether they are an interesting little party; it surely looks as if Madge and her Rex family are going places.

The Rex coat can be transferred to almost any breed of cat and it has now been discovered that Siamese can again share their unique markings with the new breed. Mrs Lidyard from Kent recently informed me that she had a 'Rexed' Siamese kitten.

In the North of England Mrs Genty has bred some Rex kittens, using Mrs Lauder's 'Belhaven Nectarine' and her own 'Ch. Cathiss Torti Queen', bred by Mrs Vickers.

The exhibition of Rex cats at the 1965 Olympia National Cat Club Show, sponsored by the Colour-Point and Any Other Variety Club, gave a great fillip and interest to these very special feline delights. Altogether there were 24 Rex cats and kittens on show, and amongst them, in a gaily decorated pen was 'Annelida Honeybun', a cream Rex owned by the Chairman of the Governing Council of the Cat Fancy, Miss Kathleen Yorke. The interest of so important a cat fancier augurs well for a quick launching of the Rex cat.

The Foreign Whites are the very newest thing in cats to be presented to the cat world. Success for this breed is anticipated because a particularly 'green-fingered' fancier, Miss Pat Turner of Loughborough, has adopted them wholeheartedly. Though Miss Turner does not give herself credit for having first discovered the Foreign Whites, in her own words she adds:

'But I do think, however, that I was the first person to see any future for them and to do anything about them'.

The recognition of these unusual cats was forced on Miss Turner when a badly-developed photograph of her Lilac queen, revealed a cat without any points or markings, Siamese in type, but white all over. Though cat fanciers were very familiar with white cats of British type, the keen eyes of Miss Turner now saw something different – a white cat of foreign type! She could not ignore this apparition, for what she saw before her was a vision too beautiful to dismiss lightly. She felt suddenly inspired to do something, and she did not let the sun go down on her ambition.

Her first step was to acquire a British White Short-hair, which at first was quite difficult to obtain. This was bred to a Lilac-Pointed Siamese, and the white female kittens from this litter were bred back again to Siamese – this time to Miss Lant's 'Beaumanor Binko'. This breeding proved to be very interesting for it showed Seal, Tortie-Point, Red-Point and Foreign Whites. Miss Turner then used her genetic knowledge and infinite care for cats for more intelligent crosses with the right kind of Siamese and the breed is now showing signs of having made the grade.

A Foreign White Cat Society has now been formed, and a standard of points has been drawn up and presented to the Colour-Point and A.O.V. Club, which club will take care of the release of the Standard of Points. Roughly, the standards mooted are that the Foreign Whites should be Siamese in type, with either blue or golden eyes and the coat should be pure white, without any markings. Membership of the Foreign White Cat Society is restricted, and all attempts to keep the breed pure are very praiseworthy. One clause, if it is enforced, will give such protection to the Foreign Whites, that they will be out on their own in the world of pedigree cats, viz.:

'I agree that sales of Foreign White stock should be

made only to those who are members of the Foreign White Society or who agree to accept its rulings'.

Miss Turner takes every opportunity to exhibit her special White 'babes' extolling their virtues and displaying their charms. In this way she has aroused the interest of the public and the press.

The Van Cat of Turkey, which aroused interest first in 1961 when Miss Lushington had them on exhibition at the National Show again in Olympia. I wrote about them in *Cats in Clover*.

'The Van Cat of Turkey, seen only on exhibition, is a complete outsider. Though not in appearance of foreign type, he has come from across the Black Sea. He is a most distinguished looking animal, with a long white coat, chestnut head, and a ringed tail, and is sure to appeal to the breeders of the unusual. Exceptionally affectionate and companionable, he may well attach himself to English fanciers as his cousins from Siam and Burma have done'.

I think he has more than justified my early hopes of his popularity for apart from his attractive appearance he has more go in him than most cats and can take to the water and swim!

In this short look at the breeds of the future there are many that I have not been able to mention. All English fanciers will know that there are breeds on the continent and abroad that are not recognized breeds in this country. But one day they will come to England. If they are handsome and agreeable we will seek them out. Membership of our great feline empire is open to all the class cats of the world.

14 Today's Persians

A Persian cat is an extremely elegant and aristocratic creature. Fifty years of selective breeding have produced an animal of rare beauty and distinction. All colours are popular today, but *The* cat of this generation is the Blue Persian.

Grace Pond, in her book on Persian Cats, has done much to popularize the Blues, as having bred all varieties for twenty years, she wrote:

'Before I started really serious breeding I had a number of varieties of Long Hairs, including Black, Brown Tabby, Silver Tabby and Blue Chinchillas. Although all these have been delightful kittens, I never found the demand for them in those days that there were for the Blue Persians, and anyone coming to buy a kitten always chose a Blue if there was one available. So I gradually cut down the number of my cats from twenty of various varieties to six of the best Blues I could afford.'

Since the Frances Simpson era great improvements have taken place in the Blue Persian cat. His coat is now of a more pleasing colour, and the contours of the face and nose have altered. The first Blue Persians were rather dark and slatey in colour, but today's cats are really blue, varying in depth according to the breeding. The long nose, so noticeable on these cats in the old cat books, is a bad feature, for the nose should be short and broad and the cheeks full. The peke-like face, so much fancied in the U.S.A., is not quite right according to our standards, though there are some breeders that applaud it, not fully understanding that the peke-like face is an uncomfortable

set-up for cats, sometimes causing running nose and eyes.
Glancing through old advertisements of stud cats, it
would seem that in the early twenties the snub-nosed Blue
Persian, and the light-coated one had begun to make a hit.
A breeder from Nuneaton writing in 1924 described her
stud cat as follows:

AT STUD
Nailstone Omar
By Buzz Buzz, has an even shade of light Blue coat.
Extremely snub-nosed and wide between ears, which
are tiny. Great wealth of bone and constitution.
Fee 15s.

ALSO HIS SON
Nailstone Shaiton
Very snub-nosed, copper eyes, tiny ears, pale Blue.
Fee to a limited number of queens 17s. 6d.

Mrs Joan Thompson, international judge and delegate
to the Governing Council, is the foremost breeder of Blue
Persians in the world. Her championship stock are found
in every corner of the globe where cats are valued. Her
magnificent Blue male, 'Champion Foxborrow Frivolous',
has sired over thirty Blue, Cream and Blue-Cream
Champions. Mrs M. Brunton, a well-known judge, Vice-
Chairman of the Governing Council, and for many years
Secretary of the National Cat Club, is also equally well-
known as a breeder of Blues. Her exports have been many,
and her records equally good. Mrs Brice Webb, Mrs
Aitken, Mrs McVady, Miss Statman, Mrs Benbow, Mrs
Crickmore are amongst the many names associated with
the breeding of the best Long-Haired Blues.

In the North, Mrs Burrow's well-known Champion
Orion of Pensford, bred by Mrs Thompson, has brightened
the scene for many Northern breeders. Mrs Lucille
Williams, the most local of the names mentioned has an
ideal Cattery and breeds some excellent light-coated Blue
Persians, many of her exports have won *Best in Show* on

the Continent. She is also the only Northern judge of Blue Persians.

A Blue Cream is one of the daintiest Long-Hairs seen today. In recent years she has improved tremendously, and the intermingling of the pastel shades of Blue and Cream has produced a cat of great beauty. For a period many cats of this breed made their appearance showing coats the colours of which did not blend artistically and were patchy, not having the shot-silk effect the breeders hoped for. For a while they lost their popularity. Also there were breeding difficulties, as Blue Creams are not bred in litters like other cats, the males being usually sterile, they are produced by mating Blue to Cream, or Cream to Blue.

The establishment of the Long-Hair Cream and Blue Cream Association in 1961 by Miss Yorke did much to create interest and promote these breeds. Mrs K. Brough, who was herself a breeder of Creams was the able Secretary, and another important breeder, Mrs Dugdale was Treasurer. The President was Miss E. Shepherd, also well known for the quality of the many champions she has bred. Though the type was good in Creams, the colour had not been well defined. The new Society made attempts to rectify this. Mrs Aitken gave her definition of creams as 'cream faintly tinged with palest primrose'. Mrs Janet Newton is a personality no fancier could overlook as she has bred many varieties for over 30 years, and who, in the cat world, has not heard of 'Champion Congo of Knott Hall' bred by the well-known judge Mr Felix Tomlinson? Mrs Knight, another well known Blue Persian breeder, has brought her 'Mooncoin Prefix' all the way from Kilkenny, and Mrs Trevitt exhibits a most beautiful Champion Blue, 'Poppet of Pensford'.

Mrs Thompson, who always thought that Blue Creams were superb, wrote of Creams in *Our Cats*:

'One respect in which Creams have improved in post-war years is that we see fewer cats with a tendency to bars on the forepaws and faint suggestions of tabby markings. This is due to the fact that their original ancestors, Red Tabbies and Tortoiseshells are becoming more remote in the pedigrees of our best Creams.'

In the North of England the Lomond Creams bred by Mrs Richardson are familiar to us, also Mrs Plews is well known for her interest in this variety. Miss Sellars has now added Blue Creams to her many other interesting breeds.

Chinchillas are a very old breed and have beautified the feline scene for over half a century. They are the smallest of the Long-Hair breeds, and have the prettiest type of face, absolutely symmetrical in its lines. It has distinctive wide-open green eyes, and its whitish coat is delicately tipped with black. These cats are possessed of great poise, hence their popularity with photographers and the television. Mrs Polden and Mrs Turney are amongst the best-known breeders, and in the North Chinchillas are now very much associated with the name of Mrs Lodge.

The Colour-Point, at one time called the Stirling-Webb cat is now well established, and improves with each succeeding generation. Mrs Watt has done much to develop this breed and her exports to the continent have proved useful in establishing the breed in new countries. Eye colour today is distinctly Siamese blue and any tendency to foreign type has disappeared. Mrs Harding is another well-known Colour-Point admirer and she, too, is working hard to develop this breed on the right lines.

In recent years Mrs Hogan has given lovers of White Persians something to talk about and revel in. Her prefix Snow White describes exactly the subject mentioned. By selective breeding and later great care given to the kittens produced, she may now compliment herself on being the breeder of the best White Persians of this decade. It is not that she has bred the odd high flyer, but her cats have been consistently good all along the line. Her Champion 'Snowwhite Giselle', in addition to being Best in Show on four other occasions, won *Best Exhibit in Show* at the National in 1964.

Tortoiseshells are still very rare. They are not positively bred but just arrive. They are very attractive, and invariably female. To arrive at the correct standard is very difficult, for they must have the three colours, black, cream and red in separate patches, without smudging. A Red Self is another uncommon variety which breeders have worked on for years but which has never really attained great popularity.

Black Persians in the North have been well taken care of by Miss Bull who breeds, in addition to many others, her famous Deebank Blacks, many of which are champions. These cats are perfect specimens and their coats are black as ink; in fact, no one has ever identified the colour black correctly in animal life until one has seen Champion 'Deebank Mascot'. Blacks are very popular in U.S.A. and in 1959 the Cat of the Year was Grand Champion 'Vel-Vene Voodoo', who was Best in Show 23 times. Voodoo set up a winning seam for Blacks and they never lost their popularity in U.S.A. Smokes, which as kittens are often mistaken for Blacks, have achieved new successes in the North through the interest and careful breeding of Mr and Mrs Leving.

Brown Tabbies are very rare and a very neglected breed, but Silver Tabbies have found in Scotland a great sponsor in Miss Mary Duff, a well-known veterinary surgeon, who sent me the following helpful notes on the now popular Tabbies.

The Long-Haired Silver Tabby

This is at once a beautiful and a charming member of the Persian family. It is to be regretted that it is not more widely known and bred in this country and not more often to be seen in our shows.

As the name indicates the Long-Haired Silver Tabby has a coat of clear, bright silver against which stand out tabby markings of dense black. The undercoat is nearly white and the texture is fine and silky. The salmon-pink nose is outlined with black as are the large, wide-open eyes, which should be green in colour. In this latter respect the Long-haired Silver Tabby differs from its Short-haired counterpart in whom green or hazel eye-colour is equally acceptable.

As with all Persians the body should be sturdy, short and cobby, low-slung on stout thick legs. The head should be broader than long with a good width between the small ears, a broad muzzle and a short nose – though this should not be so short as to resemble the nose of a Pekinese dog. The tail should be short and thick, and banded with black and silver.

In temperament the Long-haired Silver Tabby is delightful. The kittens are vivacious, full of mischief, intelligent and affectionate, purring loudly at the slightest caress. The adults are docile and companionable and will live in harmony with one another and other animals. They make ideal house cats and their coats are easier to maintain in good order than some of the other varieties of Persians.

The newly born kittens of this variety are very strikingly marked with three black lines running down the back from shoulders to root of tail and separated from one another by two silver lines of twice their breadth. Later these markings merge into a hazy silver and black and kittens of three and four months old are of an indeterminate colour. When the adult coat appears the definite tabby marks return appearing first on the shoulders in a butterfly mark then spreading down the centre of the back and up the head and finally the side markings with the flank whorl appear. To get a Long-haired Silver Tabby in complete coat for a show is no easy matter as this pattern of events is repeated with each yearly casting of coat. If the show is too early the side marks are not in, if the show is too late the back markings are blurred due to the long coat parting down the centre and falling to each side. Only for about eight weeks of the year is the coat just right. Perhaps this accounts for their scarcity in our shows.

The welfare of the breed is watched over by the Chinchilla, Silver Tabby and Smoke Cat Society the Secretaryship being in the hands of Miss Evelyn Langston, 8 Crauford Rise, Maidenhead.

15 Short-Hairs Today

Siamese

Today's Siamese cat is a very handsome animal. Years of careful breeding have eradicated many bad faults and the round head, the pronounced squint, and the unbecoming kinks have gone forever. The texture of the coat, too, has changed. The fluffiness, so noticeable a few years ago, is now replaced by a close-lying sleek fur which outlines the beautiful physique of a Siamese cat. Colouring too has improved, and foreign type is well established.

As a result of help given by skilled veterinarians, the Siamese cat has improved in health, and he is now well acclimatized to our rigorous winters. As a house trained domestic pet he has no rival, and he is so clean that he is a comfortable companion for the most fastidious.

The last few years have seen the emergence of some rare and beautiful Siamese, and the disappearance of many nondescript ones, who have entered the pet cat section now, we hope, forever. Amongst a galaxy of notable Seal-Pointed cats are Mrs Peck's world-acclaimed champions, Mrs Forrest's equally famous Dunchattons, Mrs Keene's 'new look' stars, winning at Olympia and all down the line, the famous Spotlights bred by the Warners, the Hillcross world travellers, Mrs Hindley's champions, the first of this generation, Mrs Hudson's of the classic lines, Mrs Saunder's magnificent 'Supra Cassandra', Mrs Martin and Miss Eley's Whiteoaks and Whiteacres cats, renowned for stamina and style. Bennett's very delightful Rushcrofts, Lingard's excellent Scomanessas, Bradbury's nice type Abyseals, Denny's Pi-Den Best in Show winners, Fellow's

Karamong gentile cats, Wilde's Woodhouse well-bred cats, Owen's elegant 'Sompar Matador', Watson's important Milori champions, Burness's Windale high-flyers, Wilson-Taylor's Crimplesham All-the-Time winners, Wilson's dainty Amberleys, Codrington's musical Watermills, Dunnill's Sumfun excellent cats, Haynes's famous Waverleys, Hewlett's stylish Gaywoods, Buttery's prize winning Samsaras, Kite's well-marked Lu-Chus, Macalister's typy Kualas, Conoley's quality exports, Bowers's goodlooking Siepoos, Philpot's distinguished Bitchets, Price's aristocratic Devorans and Tilby's dashing Katrines happy Hawthorns.

More and more and more! These are just a small number of the cats that will make the 1960's memorable years for Seal-Point Siamese.

The breeding of Blue-Points in any numbers did not really get on the way until the late 1940's. Major and Mrs Rendall pioneered the breed; Mrs Lauder helped considerably. Mrs Lamb's Champion 'Pincop Azure Kym' put Blue-Points on the map in the post-war era.

At first these cats were rather on the large size, but the glacial white coat, referred to in the Standard of Points, was more noticeable than it is today. Mrs Isobel North was the first breeder in Scotland to produce good Blue Points. In partnership with Mrs Murray, they made long journeys to England to show their cats. The first Scottish Champion was Laurentide Cometes, jointly owned by both these pioneer breeders. Mrs M. Smith later bred the first female Blue-Point Champion. Today, Mrs MacBeath, Mrs Saunders, Mrs Binnie and Mrs Weymouth are showing some excellent Blue and Lilac-Points.

In Newcastle, Mrs R. Mavis Dunn, owned the first post-war Blue-Point Female Champion, and later, bred a most magnificent male, Ch. 'Fenham Tarkas'. In Bradford, Mrs Bowers bred another Blue-Point Champion – 'Siepoo Azure Emperor', and Mrs Lumb, from the same Yorkshire area bred another very stylish Champion – 'Purrdale

Willow Pattern'. Miss Rickson, the first Siamese judge in the Manchester area, has bred some really outstanding Blues, amongst them Mrs Haiseldean's 'Champion Gaylord Prospero' and Mrs Chappell's 'Champion Hathor Merit' won the Champion of Champions class at Olympia, in 1965.

Mrs V. V. Bowles, another Northerner, bred the most spectacular Blue-Point in England in 1963. He was unbeaten at every show, winning more than a dozen Challenge Certificates, and several Best in Shows. Unfortunately, 'Ch. Pheenoi Fuang' died before making much mark on future generations. In the Rugby area, Mrs Macalister bred a really nice cat known as 'Champion Kuala Cynara'.

Further South Blues are very much in the news, and Mrs Biggie's 'Champion Linton Ajax', Mrs Halliday's 'Champion Safari Winston', Mrs Floyd's 'Champion Bru Bru Yogi', Miss Griffith's 'Champion Safari Casanovo' hold the brief for Blue-Points. Again Mrs Hudson, Mrs Walshe, Mrs Macaulay, Miss Turner, Mrs Philpot, Mrs Folkes and many others have exhibited some outstanding stock.

The Lilacs are Mrs Fisher's very special felines. She has bred many lovely Praha champions, including 'Champion of Champions Praha Poco Allergando'. Mrs Ashford, Mrs Sayers, Mrs Hopper, Mrs King, Miss Turner, Mrs Proudlock, Mrs Kropodra, are producing some beautiful Lilacs. A great improvement has taken place in this breed, as Lilacs are now scoring high marks for good Siamese type which was missing in the breed when first launched. The late Kathleen R. Williams was the co-founder of the Lilac Society and she herself, bred the first all-Lilac Litter.

Introducing the Lynx-Point to the North is Mrs Holt of Blackpool, who has acquired an exceptionally good cat known as Spotlight Ricky Dicky.

Chocolates, which are really one of the most attractive of the Siamese varieties, have never reached the top, and when they make strides, they cannot hold their ground.

Mrs Ashford's 'Champion Misselfore Chocolate Whey' has sired many champions, and is a great asset to the breed. Mrs Keene, Mrs Sayer, Miss Yates, Mrs Silson, Mrs Lapper, Miss Lant, Miss Turner, have exhibited some handsome Chocolates in recent months. At my first judging engagement at Croydon Show, I met a most beautiful little Chocolate kitten, bred by Mrs Silson. A slight squint marred its rise to a tip top place. I hoped that the squint might have been temporary, being caused by show fever or digestive trouble.

The overwhelming popularity of the Siamese has resulted in the establishment of so many Siamese cat clubs that if they amalgamated for their own purpose they could cut the Cat Fancy in two. The clubs which cater for all colours of Siamese are:

(1) The Siamese Cat Club
(2) The Siamese Cat Society of the British Empire
(3) The Siamese Cat Association
(4) The Northern Siamese Cat Society.

More specialized Clubs are the:
(5) The Blue-Pointed Cat Club
(6) The Chocolate-Pointed Cat Club
(7) The Lilac-Pointed Cat Club
(8) Shadow-Point Cat Club
(9) Lynx-Pointed Cat Club
(10) Foreign Whites
(11) Red-Point and Tortoiseshell Cat Club.

The latter four clubs cater for breeds as yet unrecognized, and as Siamese were used in the establishing of these breeds, it is not unreasonable to expect that they will, in the near future, come into line with the other 24 a, b and c's.

The Northern Siamese Cat Society, our own Northern Society, in which I am Co-Founder, was established at York in 1962, and it has given a great fillip to Northern breeders. The officers come from widely separated areas, Mrs E. Towe, the President from Sussex, the Vice-President, Miss G. Kent, from Blackpool, another Vice-President and Co-founder, Mrs K. Brough, from Scunthorpe, the Secretary and Treasurer, the Macalisks a cat-loving-team from Rugby, and myself, the Chairman, from Cleadon, near Sunderland. The committee are almost hand-picked and are all most interested and dedicated workers. On such strong foundations, there is every hope that the Society will survive.

Burmese

Next Short-Hair cat in order of popularity is the Burmese. They are a most exciting addition to our foreign list. During the twenty years or so of their British occupation their type has improved considerably. The Burmese Cat Club concern themselves a great deal in studying the trends of fashion that come and go with these stylish cats. They are quick to notice disfiguring faults, and try to encourage breeders to eradicate them. Top awards are withheld from Burmese cats if they resemble too closely the Siamese, especially with regard to the shape of the head, which should not be snipey. The tail should be straight not whipped, nor, of course, kinked. Eye colour has caused much controversy, and, at last, seems to be definitely fixed as yellow. Mr and Mrs Watson of Matlock who took over Burmese from Mrs France, have identified themselves with protecting the standards of the Burmese breed. Mr Watson has himself written in *Fur and Feather* about eye colour:

'The eyes of a Burmese should be yellow – a clear yellow free from greyness or any trace of muddiness . . . Daylight of reasonably high intensity (but not bright sunlight) is essential for the proper judging of Burmese eye colour. There are two good reasons for this: first, if the light is not strong the dark pupil will not be contracted and therefore the yellow iris will not be properly seen.

Secondly, yellow is a colour which is affected greatly by the colour of the light in which it is viewed.'

About the newer Blue Burmese he added:

'Blue Burmese eye colour at present tends to be rather less intense and a little greener in hue (cf. the lower intensity of the colour of Blue-Point Siamese compared with that of Seal-Point) but there are a few Blue Burmese with distinctly golden eyes. It is not unreasonable to hope that the use of these cats in breeding will result in a general upgrading of eye colour in this section of the breed.'

Mrs Waldo Lamb's 'Chinki Golden Goddess' made a great hit for Burmese when it won Best in Show in 1955. Since then, however, many beautiful Burmese appear at shows today and Mrs Silkstone, Mrs Pocock, Mrs Shrouder, Miss Macpherson, Mrs Giles, Mrs Bentinck, Mrs Merry, Mrs Towe, have bred some lovely champions. Mrs Knowles bred the first Blue Burmese champion, showing Blue Burmese for first time ever at Northern Counties Championship Show in 1960. This was immediately after the breed was recognized.

Abyssinian

The Abyssinian is a very old breed, and has been exhibited for many years. As it is not a prolific breeder, and also as females are in the minority, it will never be overcrowded. In recent years the breed has become more popular, and type has improved, but there are still too many with white chins and lockets. Though it seems to be difficult to eradicate this fault entirely some breeders are managing to keep it under control. The recognition of the Red Abyssinian has added a new and special charm to the breed. Miss Yorke, writing in *Our Cats* 1963 New Year Greeting's issue about a vision she saw in Paris said:

'Consideration for space prevents me from mentioning all the breeds in this my New Year message to you all. But I just cannot refrain from mentioning one cat I saw at a show in Paris which "took my breath away." She sat in the palms of a steward's hands as a Golden Goddess, gazing into the past of some thousand years, aloof, dignified and unperturbed, alone with her thoughts and yet surrounded by a great throng of admirers. I was spellbound to see such beauty in a living creature. She was a Red Abyssinian – and how I wished to own her! The show was the Cat Club de Paris Exhibition.'

Many of our most choice home-bred Abyssinians are exported and win high honours abroad. Mrs Towe's 'Hillcross Tawny' recently romped away with three Challenge certificates in a row and though barely adult, became an international champion. Mrs Winsor has bred and exported for many years and her 'Tranby' prefix can be discovered in many Abyssinian pedigrees. Mrs Menezes, Mrs Oswald, Mrs Earnshaw, Miss Bone, Miss Wiseman, Mrs Shrouder, Miss Macpherson, Mrs Towe, Mrs Bradbury, Mrs Macalister, are all breeders of note who have added fresh names of honour to this delightful breed. Mrs Threadingham has had the honour of breeding the very first British Red Abyssinian Champion – 'Bernina Heidi'.

Russian Blue

The Russian Blue is a very elegant foreign type cat, with many attractive traits to its character. It has been a recognized breed for many years, but lately it has fallen a little into disfavour with judges. This is probably because of variations in type. The Russian Blue Cat Club has lately gone very quiescent and the Short-Hair Cat Society is taking care of the breed. It is thought that when the club is re-started the standard of points will revert to pre-war standards, which is more in harmony with the clubs abroad. In the early thirties show catalogues contained many entries for Russian Blues.

Mrs Rochford, who died recently, and who was so well known at shows, was the foremost breeder of Russian Blues in this decade, and she it was who kept the breed alive during the difficult war years. Many spectacular Dunloes have brightened the scene. 'Premier Dunloe Pavlovitch', owned by Miss German, made his debut at Sandy Show in 1948, and soon became the best known neuter in the country, winning all along the line. The name of 'Champion Dunloe Domokvitch' occurs in many pedigrees today.

The catalogue of the National Show in 1965 contained an entry of 10 adults and 10 kittens, which shows that interest in this romantic breed is not lagging. In the North of England, the best known loyal supporter of Russian Blues, is Mrs Kirby, who has some excellent cats, including 'Champion Harvees Antimony'.

Chestnut Brown Foreign

The Chestnut Brown Foreign cat has not rocketted to any great overflowing popularity if one is to judge by classes at recent shows.

'Recently Challenge Certificates have been withheld, and this is probably because being too inbred the eye colour is losing the vivid green colour which should be a characteristic of this breed. Eye colour should be green so as to distinguish it from Burmese, and the keeping to the green eye in the standard of points was one condition of its recognition by the Governing Council. However, it is satisfactory to note that coats seem to be improving in density of colour. In our opinion this breed should have a more distinctive name.'

The death of Miss E. Von Ullman was a great loss to this breed. Mrs Clavier and Miss Warren have bred some of the best Chestnut Browns seen today. In the North Mrs P. Keith bred the first Northern champion.

Manx Cats

What is the origin of the Manx? That ever recurring question will, in all probability, never be answered. As with Siamese, only theories can be advanced on this subject. One fact will always be undisputed – they are fascinating little cats, very intelligent and affectionate, easy to keep and handle. It adds to their charm that they are not limited to colour, but may be black, white, red, parti-coloured, brown, red or silver tabby or tortoiseshell but they should conform to the standards.

Taillessness, height of its hindquarters, shortness of back, depth of flank are essential in a Manx cat, as also with them is combined the true rabbity or hopping gait. The coat is what is termed 'double' namely, soft and open like that of a rabbit, with a soft undercoat. This is essential. Great attention should be paid to roundness of rump, as round as an orange, being the ideal.

The greatest fault in Manx today seems to be lack of double coat.

Manx cats are now returning to favour. The Manx Club, founded in 1907 was incorporated with the Short Hair Cat Society in 1947. The late Miss Hill Shaw was secretary of both clubs for nearly thirty years, and her favourite cat was the Manx, of which she bred many champions. Since 1946 Manx have been seen at most of our shows. The most notable Manx in recent times was Miss Sladen's 'Champion Stoner Kate'. The Stoner family of Manx cats have attained great fame in England. Stoner Spiv's picture appeared on National Saving's posters, and he played on the London stage in Alice in Wonderland. He was a Silver Tabby with the most gloriously appealing eyes ever seen on a cat.

Today, Mrs Colville, has given her whole heart to the handsome Manx and there are now many champions brought to the fore through her patronage. Mr Christopher Wren, a relative newcomer to the Fancy, is also breeding Manx of excellent type.

Silver Tabby and Others

In the twenties and early thirties British Short-Hairs were numerous and popular. Silver Tabbies, in particular, were priced in the catalogues at prices ranging from £15 to £50. They are perhaps the most showy of the breeds. They are gentle, shy and affectionate and have 'pretty smiling faces', they seem to get on well with other cats especially Siamese, and the Silvers seem to be the only tabbies linked to famous cats of the past. In 1947 Mrs Towe was able to obtain a pedigree Short-Hair Silver Tabby from a pre-war breeder, born about 1938. She was a daughter of 'Silver Patrol' and grand-daughter of 'Silver Jim' and 'Silver Laurel'. She became known as 'Champion Hillcross Silver Lady', dam of 'Champion Hillcross Silver Flute', Miss Robson's well-known male.

Miss Bracey of Bristol, a breeder of Long-Hair Silver Tabbies acquired a Short-Hair with a really sparkling coat of jet black markings on pure silver. The breeding of this cat was unknown, but she inclined to foreign type rather than British. She produced several good kittens and with both these strains the Silvers were re-established, and, today there are many champions and good representatives of this lovely breed.

In 1953 a pedigree Silver Tabby male, 'Bellever Calchas D'acheux' was imported to England from Paris. He was the last of a famous French strain and was owned and bred by Monsieur Desbriere. Every kitten sired by 'Bellever Calchas' was a winner if shown, and in 1965 one of the last of his daughters, 'Hillcross Silver Petal' became a champion and was Best Short-Hair at the Southern Counties Show.

Red Tabbies are more numerous than Browns, and, also very beautiful with mahogany toned coats, and often have wonderful orange eyes. In 1946 a wonderful Red short-haired Tabby was shown in a Household Pet Section at a small show at Banstead. Judges were enthusiastic about her and the owner was encouraged to exhibit her. She was registered as 'Vectensian Copper Eyes' and shown in open classes and soon became a champion. Mated to a pedigree male she produced some good kittens including 'Champion

Vectensian Anaconda' who was the sire of 'Champion Barwell Cherry' and others. Good Red Tabbies seen at shows in recent years include 'Ch. Nidderdale Everest', 'Ch. Andersley Allflame', 'Ch. Tip Top', 'Ch. Killinghall Red Pyrene'.

The best known breeders of British cats of quality are Mrs Beever, Miss Robson, Mrs Towe, Mrs Thake, Mrs Johnson, Miss Codrington, Lady Glubb, Miss Pearson, Mrs Grant-Allen, Mrs Greenwood, Mrs Joan Richards, Mrs Vickers.

In the North we were very fortunate to have had a dedicated cat fancier of the new era, in the person of Miss Grace Hardman, who brought back to public image some beautiful British cats, especially Reds and Blacks. Mrs Budd, a well-known all-round judge, especially favoured the breeding of British Blues, but it was really Mrs S. Beever, a judge of British cats, who brought them into the first line of vision with innumerable Best in Show wins. These handsome cats are in great demand, for the un-initiated or newcomer to the Fancy, feels that the British Blue, more than any of the other British cats, most nearly resembles what they envisage a pedigree cat should be. Mrs Beever has some beautiful neuters, who are almost unbeaten in the Short-Hair Best in Show parade. Mrs Vickers, another Northerner, has exhibited some worth-while Blues, in addition to Rex and Tortoiseshell. Mrs Woolin favours Reds, and the late Mr Beckitt bred some of the most handsome Silver Tabbies seen in recent years. Miss Kit Wilson, one of the Cat Fancy's most distinguished personalities, added the small tribute quoted below to her judging notes on the Scottish Cat Club Show in 1966:

'Our British Short-Hairs certainly do flourish in the North. Many thanks to all who put such lovely exhibits under me.'

Nothing succeeds like success, and the story of the Cat Fancy, since its inception in 1910, has been one long success story. So enormous has been its growth, and so

Champion Tailong Kuli. Owner/breeder Mrs A. Peck

Champion Supra Cassandra.
Breeder Mrs M. Hudson
Owner Mrs Saunders

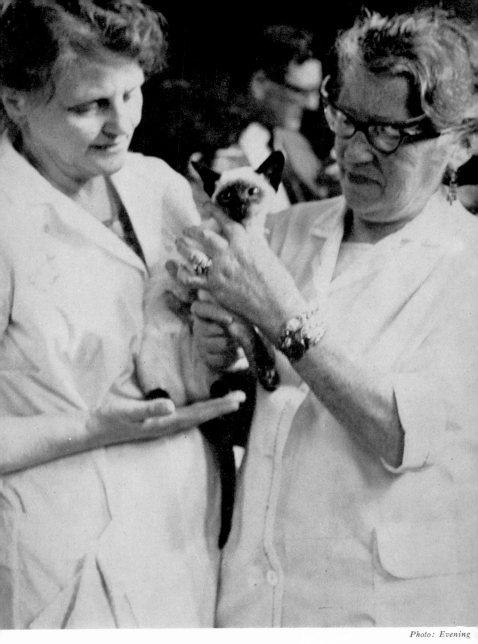

Photo: *Evening*

Judging : May Eustace (right) and steward Tess Wilson-Taylor

wide have its activities spread, that, it is certain, our successors to the field of cat history will have to write, not in books, but in volumes. I hope that many more will come after us, and that they will enjoy, as we have done, the extraordinary fascination of delving into the life of the cat.

F

16 Continental Cat Shows

Cat shows have been held by the Cat Club de Paris in Paris since 1924.

The head organization in Europe is known as the Federation International Feline European, abbreviated to F.I.F.E., to which are affiliated cat clubs in Holland, Belgium, Norway, Sweden, Denmark, Germany and Switzerland. It is associated with the Governing Council of the Cat Fancy.

From 1950 onwards other clubs were formed in Paris. The first was the Amis des Chats, followed by the Cercle Félin de Paris, and the Exposition Feline International, and offshoots of some of these Clubs operate in Belgium, Germany, Norway and Switzerland. About three years ago a very strong club, Niderlandse Verenining Van Kattevrienden was formed in Holland which has had a great success. These latter clubs are not recognised by F.I.F.E. and judges officiating for them are not invited to judge at shows sponsored by the clubs affiliated to F.I.F.E.

The Cercle Félin de Paris has grown enormously with the years. At their first show in 1952 about 50 exhibits came. By 1962 the exhibits totalled over 200.

A feature of the Continental show is the two or three day 'exposition', the last day being on a Sunday, and in Paris at least the gate is enormous, with crowds milling around the hall from midday until about six p.m.

The procedure followed is very different from the English set-up, members only exhibiting. They own their own pens, transporting them to and from the show. All cats and kittens go home overnight. No entry fees are paid and there is no prize money. All exhibits receive a certificate signed by the judge. At the end of the last day, presents are given and some of them are very beautiful and valuable. These are provided by the officers and committee members and friends. These are silver cups and medals, glass of value, pictures, vases and other interesting objects. Every exhibitor receives something and the lucky winners get several things. Exhibitors can often be seen exchanging prizes among themselves.

At the Cercle Félin de Paris shows the cat pens are very large, having doors which open wide to enable the exhibits to be taken out without trouble. The wire of the pens is gilded and the floor is usually covered with quilted nylon with curtains to match. Flower decoration is added and the whole effect is very artistic and is, of course, of great interest to the visiting public.

At a recent Cercle Félin show in Paris there were many examples of the care and attention to detail given by exhibitors. Outstanding among the exhibits was a long-haired Cream with emerald green velvet curtains and cushion, set off by deep pink roses. Another Cream was reposing on lime green velvet, the pen trimmed with orange and yellow nasturtiums. There were three long-haired Blacks together, with yellow curtains and cushions set off with vivid orange calendulas, and Blacks again, backed by shell pink drapes, decorated with sprays of apple blossom.

A very regal short-haired brown Tabby was shown with rose pink curtains and a large bowl of shaded pink hyacinths. A long-haired brown Tabby was set off by apple green nylon and a red rose. Chinchillas were exhibited with apple green drapes trimmed with trails of mauve wisteria. There was also a very good Seal-Point Siamese with royal blue backing whose pen was decorated with primulas in mauve, pink and lavender. Some long-haired Blues were resplendent with white satin curtains glittering with diamanté. A Chinchilla shared her pen with a tame pigeon and they appeared to be very good friends. The pen floor had an artificial grass mat adorned with branches and leaves. A complacent Tortoiseshell sat in a miniature garden complete with rustic summer-house with various birds and small animals scattered about.

The cats and kittens are chosen for the best in show on Saturday and occupy the 'Best in Show' pens all day on Sunday, again very beautifully decorated.

Another feature of the Cercle show is the special exhibition of rescued cats organised by Dr and Madame Mery. Their organisation has carried out wonderful work for the unwanted cats of Paris and some of the exhibits are really lovely. Most of the rescued cats are neutered, given names and shown in the organisation's own pens. Little notes are placed on the pens saying 'I am Minette, I am four months old, will you give me a kind home', or 'I am Bobbette and three years old, can I live with you' and so on. Usually about thirty of these cats come to a show and by the end of the third day most have found good homes, a small charge being made to help with the funds. A basket is lent and the abandoned kitten is taken away by people who really want a pet. I have seen quite a few really lovely short-haired brown Tabbies which, but for our quarantine laws, I would have been only too pleased to have brought home.

A Spanish organisation also has a small exhibition of rescued cats at some of the Cercle Shows, and judging follows a different pattern. Exhibits are brought to the judge's table by stewards who follow a plan of the hall. Cats are not penned according to the breed numbers as ours are, so that it is very difficult to find a particular exhibit in the hall as those belonging to any one exhibitor are penned together irrespective of their breed, thus a long-haired Blue, an Abyssinian and a Siamese may be in line together. If a judge wishes to have a look at a few exhibits it is better to take the hall plan with one;

personally I like to see the cats in their pens and also by so doing one can get to know the exhibitors.

At a recent show held in Paris by the Federation International Feline Club a Kinkajou was on exhibition. This little animal was really wonderful, standing on his hind legs drinking orange juice from a glass for the amusement and interest of the public. A female Genet was also on show.

Long-haired cats are the favourites with Continental breeders and it is a joy to be given a class of eight or ten long-haired white adults, and the same number of kittens. This applies to the long-haired Blacks of which there are many. There is always a good representation of long-haired Creams, Chinchillas, Red Tabbies, Torties and Tortie and Whites, etc. Colour-Points are occasionally seen but type is not always good, the nearest to the Colour-Points being called Kymers. There are several Birman breeders and since I first saw these cats in 1951 I have admired them. They are in a special class as their coat is not completely long or completely short. They have pale silky coats, blue eyes and seal or blue masks, legs and tail, all four feet should be white, giving the appearance of wearing white slippers on the front feet while the back legs appear to be wearing white boots, part of which must extend up the back of the leg and must be evenly marked. Judges are asked to pay great attention to the 'Boots' as they must not be broken by dark toes.

The origin of the 'Sacred Cat of Burma' like our own Siamese is unknown, but they are a fascinating breed, with very sweet and gentle dispositions. Mrs Elsie Fisher has recently imported three Birmans. They have been on exhibition at a few shows and created much interest.

Siamese are not very numerous but are of much better type than formerly. Short, kinked tails and round eyes are gradually disappearing and coat and eye colour is good. The importation of a few good cats from England has helped to effect the change. A few good Short-hairs turn up at the shows, the odd Burmese, Red-Point or short-haired Blue called Chartreux. A male has recently been imported from Brussels by Mrs Beever as an outcross for our British Blues. Before the war there were some good short-haired Silver Tabbies in Paris bred by Monsieur and Madame Desbrèire. I was lucky to be able to buy the last male of the line in 1954. I gave him to Mrs K. Regan (a Silver Tabby breeder) who paid for his quarantine and registered him with her prefix 'Bellever' which form of registration was allowed at that time. 'Calchas' was subsequently transferred to me as Mrs Regan was unable to keep him.

He was at stud for several years and was an excellent outcross for our inbred Silvers. All kittens sired by him, if shown, were prize winners and he helped to lay the foundation of the strain of lovely Silver Tabbies we see in the shows today.

At the Cat Club de Paris Show at the Salle Hoche on 3rd and 4th April, 1937 two Silver Tabby kittens of 'Calchas' strain were first in their respective classes. Their owner, Madame Desbrière received the Prix d'Honneur offered by the President of the French Republic for the best European kittens.

I bought 'Calchas' on Miss Langston's advice as she had seen the Desbrière cats winning at shows in Paris for many years. All were pure bred and were registered with the Cat Club de Paris.

Abyssinians were quite well established in Paris before the war, due again to English imports, notably Championship Woodroffe Zeus. Mademoiselle Rose Meyer showed about a dozen at the Amis des Chats Show in 1951. They were in an enormous pen, the floor being covered with golden sand with large rocks placed here and there. The top and sides of the pen were lined with thin green silk and with a clever lighting arrangement the whole effect was of small lions reclining in the desert.

Recently Madame Heyer of the Cercle Félin Club

imported a good male Abyssinian from America and two
from England, now known as 'Champion Taishun Tula'
and 'Champion Hillcross Tawny'. From these cats she is
building up a very good strain of Abyssinian with excellent type and colour. They attract great attention when
shown reclining on pale yellow cushions.

The Dutch Club (Niderlandse Verenigning Van Kattevrienden) has carried out a great deal of experimental
breeding. They have good Chocolate and Lilac Persians;
a standard of points has been drawn up and is strictly
adhered to. The long-haired Chocolate exhibited at a
Paris Show was of sound even colour and the Lilac had a
really lavender coat. I have not seen any so good in this
country. Chestnut Brown Foreigns are also very popular
in Holland. There is always something interesting at the
Continental shows, making the admission charge of 2 to 3
francs worthwhile.

17 Reflections on Cat Shows from 1920 to the Present Day

When the cat shows started again in 1920 after the Great War, it was inevitable that changes would be made. One of the first apparent changes was in the dress of judges. In the earliest shows overalls seemed to have been unknown, for men judged in frock coats and ordinary suits and women in elaborate, long-skirted, long-sleeved dresses. Photographs show men wearing straw and bowler hats and women in Ascot-type headgear at both indoor and outdoor shows. The penning of the cats was very little varied, but a great improvement had taken place regarding the comfort of the cats which were then provided with blankets and sanitary pans. Judges appeared to have adopted overalls and the use of disinfectant. The age of kittens was raised from eight to nine months, and it became compulsory to avoid any distinguishing marks.

From 1920 until the next war in 1939, shows seem to have followed a more or less uneventful pattern. A few new clubs were formed including South Western Counties and Southsea, but the shows were held in small halls, the Kitten Show in the Porchester Hall, the Siamese Show in the Philbeach Hall. The Midland Club held their Shows at various places, Cheltenham, Gloucester and Worcester. The first Blue Persian Show was held in London in 1933. The highlight of the year was the national Cat Club's two-day Show at the Crystal Palace in early December. In 1936 however, the Crystal Palace was burned down only two days before the great event, and Mrs Sharman, the Show Manager, performed herculean feats to present this show. A new venue was found at once at the Paddington Baths. All exhibitors were sent telegrams advising them of the change. Spratts, the penning firm, were notified, judges and stewards were alerted, and the Show opened as usual on the correct day, but for one day only. The National Cat Club has not so far reverted to the two-day show. The Crystal Palace was never re-built and the Club continued with a one-day show at Paddington Baths until December 1938 when once again all shows were stopped because of the world situation and did not start again until 1945.

When showing was resumed the system of sending cats unaccompanied by rail was soon discontinued, also the feeding of exhibits at Shows by the Club helpers.

The first important show was held at the end of 1945 by the Notts and Derby Cat Club. This drew a big entry, especially of Siamese, but unfortunately an outbreak of cat distemper laid almost all the exhibits low within a week and sad to recall, most did not survive. This was a great tragedy, as at that time we had no vaccine to help in any way, no penicillin or the other wonder drugs that we now take so much for granted. Many of us were short of fuel and found it difficult to keep our houses warm, electricity cuts were frequent and all this during a particularly hard winter. It was impossible to get M and B tablets but even these did not help this severe illness at all. No more Shows were held until October 1946, when the Siamese Cat Club staged its first post war show, at Lime Grove Baths, Hammersmith. This was a great success and here one of the first Lilac-Points made her appearance. Her name was 'Larchwood Lilac', bred by Miss Kennedy Bell and owned by Mrs Hindley and she soon became a Champion. The first Lilac-Points were judged as Blue-Points until they received a breed number in 1961. The Croydon Cat Club followed with an all breed Championship Show the following month at the Croydon Baths.

Miss Adams, Miss Dixon and Mr Yeates were amongst the judges. There were about 160 exhibits and the Club thought the entry excellent. One can judge how the fancy and interest in shows has grown when we compare the entry to over 400 exhibits in 1966.

The National Club resumed their shows with a modest entry and in no time at all were staging their annual event in the National Hall, Olympia. The Southern Counties, Midland, Kitten and Neuter Show, Yorkshire, and others resumed their shows. Several new clubs were formed who ran shows all leading up to the present great interest in cats. All started off with small halls and all are now holding their shows in bigger and better halls.

In 1950 a cat exhibition was held in the National Hall, Olympia, London. It was the first all-cat show to be held there and was sponsored by Mr Macdonald and managed by Mr A. Towe and was called the Crystal Show. Nothing had been seen like this Show before or since. The Governing Council of the Cat Fancy gave permission for their judges to officiate. Cats were shown on both days of the two-day event, most were taken home overnight and kittens appeared on the second day only. Most of the pens were decorated, cats wore smart collars or ribbon bows round their necks, the pens were sprayed with silver or gold lacquer and looked marvellous. There was a double row of Long-haired and Short-haired Champions on show, all in decorated pens and many large silver trophies were given by the Show's Patron, Christabel Lady Aberconway. Over the two days about twelve thousand people queued to see the Show. It got wide publicity and really brought cats to the notice of the public after the war. As the shows became bigger and more numerous, various improvements were introduced until gradually the shows were run as they are today.

It has been said by many people that the English system of judging is the fairest and most comprehensive in the world and English judges are in great demand to officiate at foreign shows. There are some innovations that appeal to me.

I like the Australian method of lining the pens with white cotton curtains. A show was held in 1962 in England using this method and although many people professed themselves against it, the exhibitors and public loved the idea, as one lady said, 'The Show sparkles' and the curtains certainly camouflaged the often dreary looking wire pens. Coloured curtains are often used for decorated pens for cats on exhibition only and are very effective although they cannot compete with the decorated pens at some of the Continental shows.

In 1945–6–7 about eight to ten judges would be used, gradually being increased until twenty years later it is usual for some all breed championship shows to engage twenty and more judges. This applies mostly to shows held in London or big northern cities.

From 1950 onwards the Crystal Cat Club staged two more exhibitions at Olympia but neither came up to the standard or excitement of the first. A Festival Show was held by the Kitten Club during the Festival of London year and was a marvellous event. Championships were given at this Show by special permission of the Governing Council.

The Governing Council of the Cat Fancy organised an all breed Show in 1953 to celebrate the Coronation of Her Majesty, Queen Elizabeth. It was held in the Horticultural New Hall at Westminster and was run by Mr A. Towe. This was a very grand affair and was presided over by Miss Yorke, the Chairman of the Governing Council. Several Continental judges officiated and gifts for prizes were received from all the Continental clubs. The Marchioness of Carisbrooke, Christabel Lady Aberconway and Mr Beverley Nichols were among the notables present to make speeches and present prizes and rosettes.

The next show organised by the Governing Council was held in September 1960 to celebrate the Golden

Jubilee of the Governing Council. This was held in the National Hall, Olympia, and again run by Mr A. Towe. All the trophies from the most important clubs were on show, guarded by the law. They looked most impressive and wonderful prizes were again offered. All the rosettes were golden and the Best in Show pens were sprayed with golden lacquer and lined with golden paper. Some Continental judges again officiated and the Show was a great financial success.

From 1951 clubs began to stage their shows in larger halls, the Croydon, National and Southern Counties held several at the Seymour Hall and it is now the regular venue for the Siamese Cat Club Show.

The Yorkshire County Cat Club held championship shows at the Corn Exchange, Leeds for several years; the Midland Club adopted Birmingham as their permanent venue; the Notts and Derby Club held championship shows in either Nottingham or Derby; Hertfordshire and Middlesex Club started in a small hall in Watford but for a few years now have had their championship show at the Alexandra Palace, London. This is a most pleasant place to hold a show for the grounds are lovely and the view over London and the surrounding country is unsurpassed. The Croydon Cat Club, which held its first championship show in 1920, and the Kitten and Neuter Club and the Southern Counties Club have all moved to the Horticultural Hall, Westminster. In 1957 the old Northern Counties Cat Club was revived and held their first post war championship show at Seaburn, and in 1960 an exhibition of cats was held in a marquee at the Sunderland Flower Show creating great interest and making a profit of nearly one hundred pounds, thus enabling the Club to engage the Palatine Hotel, Sunderland for their next championship show. This was a very unusual type of venue. The cats were penned in a modern ballroom carpeted with tartan, the curtains and other furnishings were also of tartan and even the Club rosettes were of the same Black Watch tartan. Unfortunately this old Club did not receive the support due to it and in spite of the efforts of Mr and Mrs Foster, Mrs R. M. Dunn and Mrs Eustace in particular, the Club has not been able to hold a show for a few years. Fortunately the Yorkshire Cat Club has had better luck and now holds championship shows in the Valley Gardens Pavilion, Harrogate, another very delightful venue.

The Scottish Club holds delightful shows in the Art Gallery, Sauchiehall Street, Glasgow. A special feature of the show is the household pet classes and this Club has done much good work for unwanted cats. Edinburgh also holds championship shows and in 1965 Aberdeen held its first cat show. This was well attended and was a huge success. In 1964, the West of England and South Wales Society held the first cat show in Wales. So far no championship show has been staged in Northern Ireland. There are many others, South Western Championship Show in Exeter, Preston Club Show at Blackpool, Coventry and Leicester Club holds shows alternatively in Coventry and Leicester, Lancs and North Western Club at Preston, Southport and Bolton, Cheshire Club at Chester, Southsea at Southsea and the Wessex at Bournemouth. The Norfolk and Suffolk held their first championship show in 1966 at Norwich. Apart from these championship shows there are many sanction and exemption shows held up and down the country, such as at Brighton, Salisbury, Reading, Bingley, Halifax, Canterbury and Bedford, so it is easy for anyone interested to exhibit or visit a cat show somewhere.

Show Season 1966

A general improvement in the type and quality of cats and kittens exhibited was noticeable during 1965–66 show season. Two special points occurred to me:

1. The popularity of the Lilac-Point Siamese and the Burmese.

2. The deterioration of some of the Seal-Point Siamese, particularly in coat colour with a few notable exceptions. However, at the end of the season a marvellous class of Seal-Point males appeared at the Wessex Cat Club's Championship Show. I hope this was a happy omen for the future as a good type Seal-Point with dense mask and points, oriental eyes and the desirable light body colour is a very handsome animal; one thinks with sadness of the good cats of both sexes which have died during the past two or three years.

It would seem that Blue and Chocolate-Points, as well as the Lilac-Points, are increasing in popularity. Many have beautiful light coats, notably the Chocolate-Points, but they have very variable masks and points. The square jaw and pinched muzzle have been largely eliminated but some Siamese now have a tendency to undershot jaws. This is a bad fault especially in females, as if the teeth cannot meet they must experience difficulty in dealing with the birth of kittens.

Although eye colour in general is superb, the true oriental shape is too often lacking.

British Short-hairs generally are excellent for type and coat pattern; although the texture of coat in some British Blues is too soft.

Silver and Red Tabbies, Tortie and Whites and Manx were to be seen at most shows, with a few good Blacks, Whites and Tortoiseshells. Cream and Brown Tabbies seem to have declined unfortunately and need to be brought back. The Short-haired Cat Society has been able to obtain the re-recognition of spotted and bi-colour breeds and has submitted a revised standard of points to the Governing Council for approval. Foreign Short-hairs are doing well, some of the Abyssinians are excellent, also the Burmese, particularly the Browns, the required yellow eye colour is more evident, but I do not think the coat colour of the Blue Burmese is as good as it used to be.

The Russian Blues are again gaining in popularity and

the Short-haired Cat Society, after consultation with breeders, is submitting a revised Standard of Points to the Governing Council and it is hoped that this breed will again reach its former popularity. Chestnut Brown Foreign cats are very limited here but seem very popular on the Continent.

Much interest is shown in the new breeds. Lynx or Shadow-Points, Red and Tortie-Pointed, Rex, Foreign Short-haired Whites and the lovely imported Birmans. Progress is good but it is hoped that interest will not decline in our superlative older breeds.

Long-haired cats are really lovely but it would be nice if all the colours were better represented, Whites for instance being in short supply. Before the war they were extensively bred by Mrs Peggy Cattermole of Lotus prefix fame and some lovely specimens were shown by Mrs Cox Ife and Captain St Barbe. Mrs Durbin and Miss Seller have good ones today. Long-hairs used to be the most popular and the most photographed. They certainly need more attention than the short-haired variety as it is essential for their health and well being that their long fur be brushed and combed daily; if allowed to knot and tangle it is difficult to carry out the necessary grooming. Probably the popularity of the short-hair cat has increased because they do not need so much attention, although we are glad to see that owners of Short-Hairs are realising that they do need grooming and show preparation as so much dead hair can accumulate in their coat, particularly at the base of the spine, making the fur appear dull and lustreless. They should be brushed and combed daily. With the short-hair coat, it should not be an arduous task.

Cats and kittens, whether long-haired or short-haired are beautiful, interesting, fascinating, demanding, arrogant, possessive, maddening and affectionate. We have no favourites. We love all cats.

APPENDIX 1

Modern Veterinary Treatment

By M. Duff, MRCVS

The wind of change blows strongly and it has stirred to the very roots the field of Veterinary Science. In the past quarter of a century great advances have been made in every aspect of veterinary treatment including that of the cat.

Probably the biggest single forward step came when Sir Alex Fleming discovered the bacteriocidal properties of the Penicillin fungus. This discovery started a long programme of research which resulted in the range of antibiotics we know today – penicillin, streptomycin, aureomycin, terramycin, chloromycetin etc.

The cat has benefited from these antibiotics. Before they were known abcesses, many of them caused by bites from other cats, were difficult to heal and when bone was involved as well as muscle they frequently became chronic or healed only after months of treatment and with deformity of limb. The antibiotics have changed all this. Now, if treatment is given early enough, no abscess forms at all and even cases which have already become septic can usually be cleaned and healed in a very short time.

The antibiotics are effective too against feline pneumonia, catarrh, influenza, infectious enteritis, diarrhoea, gastritis, conjunctivitis, cystitis and other inflammatory conditions of bacterial origin. Each antibiotic has its own special use.

Older than the antibiotics but still in daily use are the

177

'sulpha drugs' the best known in the veterinary field being 693. These also have a wide range of use from pneumonia to wound dressings and eye ointments. They are frequently used in conjunction with the antibiotics since in many cases the partnership of the two gives more speedy destruction of the bacteria involved.

The antibiotics and the sulpha drugs must have saved thousands of cat's lives in recent years.

Then there are the hormones. These have various uses, some combating sterility, some toning-up the aged animal when his glandular secretions have become inadequate, some improving skin and hair. The most recent hormone to be brought into the service of man and animals is cortisone and its allied products.

Cortisone combats stress and is used in animals which have suffered injury on the road. It also allays skin irritation and is used both by injection and in the form of ointments and salves for skin conditions in cats. Another use is the relief of pain in fibrositis, arthritis and sprains.

For mismated queens stilboestral is used and given early enough it prevents conception. It does, however, lengthen the 'calling' period, in some cases prolonging it by six or eight weeks.

Of vaccines there is but one in general use for cats that for Feline Infectious Enteritis. It has been a great boon to cat fanciers most of whom have all their kittens innoculated from two to three months old. Innoculated kittens have a high immunity to this deadly complaint which used to wipe out whole catteries.

As there has been great progress on the medical side so has there been also on the surgical side. Spaying of female cats is an everyday occurrence and Caesarean births no rarity while butchers' string is frequently removed from the intestines where the knotted end has caused an obstruction. Long bones, such as leg bones, are operated upon to bring the broken ends together and fix them with a steel pin.

Nor has the geriatric cat been neglected. Injections and tablets are now available to him to assist his failing digestion, reduce his blood pressure and give him a further spell of happy life before he is gathered to his forefathers.

A health service for animals has been discussed recently so perhaps tomorrow's cat will wear contact lenses in his eyes and have National Health teeth.

APPENDIX 2

Notes on Breeding

By R. G. Turner, MA, BSC, AINSP
Lecturer in Physics Rutherford College of Technology

Some Notes on Line Breeding of Cats

It is commonly thought that line breeding, or indeed the mating of two closely related individuals, while it may be successfully pursued in the case of some livestock, is something which just must not be done in the case of cats. It is quite true that at the moment, continued unselective line breeding in any breed of cat would probably produce some unfortunate results, but I should like to point out how a carefully planned programme of this type could result in great overall improvement in the general standard of the breed.

It is the ultimate object of every breeder of cats to obtain litters in which every individual is identical and perfect in the sense that each conforms precisely with the appropriate standard of points and could not be faulted in any feature whatsoever. Each characteristic of an animal is determined initially by the genetic make-up which it inherits from its parents (with possible later modifications due to its subsequent treatment which will not be passed on to its offspring). Thus if two such perfect animals with identical genetical make-up were mated, the resulting litter would consist of similarly perfect identical individuals except that any undesirable features carried by the parents in a recessive form (and therefore not showing in the parents) would show in some of the litter. To avoid this happening it will be necessary to specify that a perfect strain of cat does not carry any such recessive factors. In addition an individual will occasionally be found to have undergone a spontaneous genetical change and will need to be weeded out from the strain.

Having defined the situation which we are trying to create, let me say at once that making each cat genetically identical would certainly not mean that each cat loses its individual character. The disposition of a cat (and to a small extent some of its physical features) will certainly be influenced by the treatment it receives after birth although its genetical make-up will not be influenced in this way. The problem then is to obtain a pair of identical genetically perfect cats free from undesirable recessive factors from which to breed similar animals. The present practice of mating cats indiscriminately simply because the stud is a champion or has a number of champions in his immediate ancestry is certainly not going to bring this about. The only way to purify a strain of any animal (that is to make the genetical make-up of individuals the same) is to mate brother to sister (or parent to offspring) and to continue doing this. Any outcross at any stage would only tend to reverse the process.

Outcrosses would be necessary from time to time during the process of establishing the strain as mentioned below, but once a perfect strain has been established an outcross would be disastrous if the offspring were allowed to mate with the pure-bred members. Of course any such line breeding programme must be pursued with some care. The final strain is gradually established by careful selection in each generation. The animals to be used for breeding are determined by examination of their first few litters rather than the animals themselves since it is only on the offspring that the effects of recessive genes become apparent.

As mentioned above, it is almost certain that, at various stages in the programme, defects will appear that are clearly carried in a recessive form by the whole strain. These must be eradicated one at a time, by one, and only one, outcross in each case. The offspring of this mating are then mated among themselves and some of these second generation animals will be free of the gene in question and may be used to continue the line breeding programme. In this way such recessive defects may be eliminated one by one, remembering always that the breeding animals are selected by consideration of their first few litters rather than by the characteristics of the animals themselves.

If such a line breeding programme is rigorously pursued (with occasional outcrosses when necessary) the final result will be a pure strain of cat, having every desirable feature and no undesirable ones which will breed true apart from occasional individuals who suffer spontaneous genetical changes. Such changes will only show in the second generation from the individual in question and so a rather careful watch would need to be kept in order to discard the impure animals for breeding purposes.

In all the establishment of a pure strain of cats in the way we have been considering would clearly be a long and costly process and quite beyond the means of most cat breeders. It is, however, to my mind, the only way in which real progress can be made in the cat breeding world. The present system of indiscriminate matings produces champions on the basis of the laws of chance, a correctly pursued line-breeding programme would eventually produce them as a matter of course.

What are Genes?

Most fanciers know that inherited characteristics are passed from parents to progeny by way of things called genes, but how many know anything more about genes? Let us try to see, in the simplest way, what they are and how they behave.

To start with, genes are minute particles, each of a

certain chemical composition, which are found in the cells of which an animal is composed. The genes in a cell are arranged in pairs and each cell, with certain exceptions, has an identical set of genes. The exceptions are those cells, used in reproduction, which have only one of each pair of genes. The fusion of two such cells, one from the male and the other from the female, produces a single cell with the full number of genes which, in the fullness of time, develops into a complete animal. Thus an animal gets half of its genes (one of each pair) from each of its parents.

Now, each pair of genes has a specific job to do. In the cat for instance, a particular pair is responsible for determining whether its coat is to be short or long, another pair for deciding whether it is Siamese, and so on. What happens, is that these genes can exist in two or more different forms, differing chemically from each other. It is often difficult to detect the effect of an individual gene or pair of genes. Many features of a cat (for instance its size or general shape) are influenced by a large number of gene-pairs and a change in any one of these pairs may have an insignificant effect. Some features, however, such as the coat colour and the pattern of any markings, are largely determined by a small number of gene-pairs, often only one, and the inheritance of such features is easily understood.

Take for instance, the pair of genes responsible for the Siamese coat pattern. If both genes of the pair have their normal form, which we will call n, the cat will be non-Siamese. If both have a certain chemical modification (we will call these genes s) the cat will be Siamese. (Geneticists use other symbols but n and s are convenient for our purpose.) If one gene of the pair is n and the other s, the influence of the n gene will override the s gene and the cat will be non-Siamese. Such a cat however, will pass on the s gene to about half of its progeny. We might say that the cat 'carries the Siamese factor'.

We do not always find this dominance of one form of a gene over the other. There is another gene pair, for instance, which determines whether a cat's coat is to be red or black. In this case a cat having one gene of each sort is partly red and partly black, the colour we call tortoiseshell. The important thing however, is that when we are talking about a single feature which is determined by a single gene-pair such as the Siamese coat pattern, there are only three possibilities. The cat is either Siamese and can only pass on s genes to its progeny or it is purely non-Siamese and can only pass on n genes or it 'carries the Siamese factor' and will pass on n and s genes in approximately equal proportions. It is nonsense, for instance, to refer to a cat as being a quarter Siamese.

I have tried here to give some idea of the basis of gene inheritance. All sorts of questions have been left un-answered. Why are essentially all tortoiseshell cats female? Why are there not two different sorts of tabby-pointed Siamese cats, silver-tabby pointed and brown-tabby pointed? Why are all red cats tabby? Why do blue eyes nearly always go with the Siamese coat pattern? The answers to these and many other questions are quite simple but can only be understood by reading an elementary textbook on genetics. So far as I know, there is no satisfactory book of this sort dealing with cats specifically. This need not however, stop one from studying the subject, the principles of genetics are universal, applying to all living things.

APPENDIX 3

Breed Numbers and Official Standards of Points

As drawn up by the Specialist Clubs and Societies, affiliated to the Governing Council Of The Cat Fancy and approved 1961.

With Additions supplied by the Clubs and Societies catering for The New Breeds, and approved by the Governing Council of the Cat Fancy 1966 and 1967.

New Breeds on the list are marked with an *.

Breed Numbers

LONG-HAIRED CATS

1	Black	9	Red Tabby
2	White (Blue Eyes)	10	Chinchilla
2a	White (Orange Eyes)	11	Tortoiseshell
3	Blue	12	Tortoiseshell-and-White
4	Red Self	*12a	Bi-Coloureds
5	Cream	13	Blue Cream
6	Smoke	13a	Any Other Colour
7	Silver Tabby	13b	Colourpoint
8	Brown Tabby	*13c	Birmans

SHORT-HAIRED CATS

14	White (Blue Eyes)	19	Red Tabby
14a	White (Orange Eyes)	20	Brown Tabby
15	Black	21	Tortoiseshell
16	Blue British	22	Tortoiseshell-and-White
16a	Blue Russian	23	Abyssinian
17	Cream	*23a	Red Abyssinian
18	Silver Tabby	24	Seal-Pointed Siamese

24a	Blue-Pointed Siamese	*30	Spotted
24b	Chocolate-Pointed Siamese	*31	Bi-coloured
24c	Lilac-Pointed Siamese	*32	Tabby-Point Siamese
25	Manx	*32a	Red-Point Siamese
26	Any Other Variety	*32b	Tortie-Point Siamese
27	Burmese	*32c	Any Other Dilution
27a	Blue Burmese	*33	Cornish Rex
28	Blue Cream	*33a	Devon Rex
29	Chestnut Brown Foreign		

STANDARDS FOR LONG-HAIRS

(1) Black – Long-Hairs

Colour. Lustrous raven black to the roots, and free from rustiness, shading, white hairs, or markings of any kind.

Coat. Long and flowing on body, full frill and brush, which should be short and broad.

Body. Cobby and massive, without being coarse, with plenty of bone and substance, and low on the leg.

Head. Round, and broad, with plenty of space between the ears, which should be small, neat, and well covered, short nose, full cheeks and broad muzzle.

Eyes. Large, round and wide open, copper or deep orange in colour, with no green rim.

N.B. Black L.-H. Kittens are often a very bad colour up to five or six months, their coats being grey or rusty in parts, and sometimes freely speckled with white hairs. Fanciers should not condemn them on this account if good in other respects, as these Kittens frequently turn into the densest Blacks.

Scale of Points

Colour	..	..	..	..	25
Coat	..	..	..	..	20
Body	..	..	..	..	20
Head	..	..	..	..	20
Eyes	..	..	..	..	15
		Total		..	100

(2) Blue-eyed White-Long-Hairs

Colour. Pure white, without mark or shade of any kind.

Coat. Long and flowing on body, full frill and brush, which should be short and broad; the coat should be close and soft and silky, not woolly in texture.

Body. Cobby and massive, without being coarse, with plenty of bone and substance, and low on the leg.

Head. Round and broad, with plenty of space between the ears, which should be small, neat and well covered, short nose, full cheeks and broad muzzle.

Eyes. Large, round and wide open, deep blue in colour.

(2a) Orange-Eyed Whites

Points as above except for eye-colour, which should be orange or copper.

N.B. Whites are very liable to get yellow stains on their tails from accumulated dust, etc. This very damaging peculiarity should be carefully attended to and stains removed before showing.

Scale of Points

Colour	..	..	..	25
Coat	..	..	..	20
Body	..	..	..	20
Head	..	..	..	20
Eyes	..	..	..	15
	Total	..		100

(3) Blue – Long-Hairs

Coat. Any shade of blue allowable, sound and even in colour: free from markings, shadings, or any white hairs. Fur long, thick and soft in texture. Frill full.

Head. Broad and round, with width between the ears. Face and nose short. Ears small and tufted. Cheeks well developed.

Eyes. Deep orange or copper: large, round and full, without a trace of green.

Body. Cobby, and low on the legs.

Tail. Short and full, not tapering (a kink shall be considered a defect). Members should not be deterred from showing their cats if they do not come up to the high standard set forth in the above definition.

Scale of Points

Coat	..	..	..	..	20
Condition	..	..	..	..	10
Head	..	..	..	..	25
Eyes	..	..	..	..	20
Body	..	..	..	..	15
Tail	..	..	..	..	10
			Total	..	100

(9) Red Tabby – Long-Hairs

Colour and Markings. Deep, rich red colour, markings to be clearly and boldly defined, continuing on down the chest, legs and tail.

Coat. Long, dense, and silky tail short and flowing : no white tip.

Body. Cobby and solid, short thick legs.

Head. Broad and round, small ears, well set and well tufted, short broad nose, full round cheeks.

Eyes. Large and round, deep copper colour.

Scale of Points

Coat	..	..	..	..	50
Body	..	..	..	..	15
Head	..	..	..	..	20
Eyes	..	..	..	..	15
			Total	..	100

(4) Red Self-Long-Hairs

Colour. Deep rich red, without markings.

Coat. Long, dense and silky, tail short and flowing.

Body. Cobby and solid, short thick legs.

Head. Broad and round, small ears well set and well tufted, short broad nose, full round cheeks.

Eyes. Large and round, deep copper colour.

Scale of Points

Coat	..	..	..	..	50
Body	..	..	..	..	15
Head	..	..	..	..	20
Eyes	..	..	..	..	15
			Total	..	100

(5) Cream-Long-Hairs

Colour. To be pure and sound throughout without shading or markings.

Coat. Long, dense and silky, tail short and flowing.

Body. Cobby and solid, short thick legs.

Head. Broad and round, small ears well set and well tufted, short broad nose, full round cheeks.

Eyes. Large and round, deep copper colour.

Scale of Points

Colour Pale to Medium	..	..	30
Coat and condition	..	..	..	20
Body	..	..	..	..	15
Head	..	..	..	..	20
Eyes	..	..	..	..	15
		Total	..	100

(11) Tortoiseshell – Long-Hairs

Colour. Three colours, black, red and cream, well broken into patches; colours to be bright and rich and well broken on face.

Coat. Long and flowing, extra long on frill and brush.

Body. Cobby and massive, short legs.

Head. Round and broad, small, well placed and well tufted ears, short broad nose, full round cheeks.

Eyes. Large and round, deep orange or copper.

Scale of Points

Coat	..	..	..	..	50
Body	..	..	..	..	15
Head	..	..	..	..	20
Eyes	..	..	..	..	15
			Total	..	100

(12) Tortoiseshell-and-White – Long-Hairs

Colour. The three colours, black, red and cream, to be well distributed and broken and interspersed with white.

Coat. Long and flowing, extra long on brush and frill.

Body. Cobby and massive, short legs.

Head. Round and broad, small, well placed and tufted ears, short broad nose, full round cheeks.

Eyes. Large and round, deep orange or copper.

Scale of Points

Coat	..	..	..	..	50
Body	..	..	..	..	15
Head	..	..	..	..	20
Eyes	..	..	..	..	15
			Total	..	100

(12a) Bi-coloured – Long-Hairs

Points

Colour. Black and White, Blue and White, Orange and White, Cream and White. No tabby shadings in the self coloured portion   20

Marking. The self colour, i.e. black, blue, orange or cream, to start immediately behind the shoulders round the barrel of body, and to include tail and hind legs, leaving the hind feet white. Ears and mask of face also self coloured. White shoulders, neck, forelegs and feet, chin, lips and blaze up face and over top of head, joining or running into the white at back of skull, thus dividing the mask exactly in half. The markings to follow those of a Dutch marked rabbit as closely as possible   ..   25

Eyes. Copper, orange or amber   5
Head. Broad and round, as in all long-hairs   ..   25
Body. Cobby and massive, short legs   25

Total   ..   100

(13) Blue Cream – Long-Hairs

Colour and Markings. To consist of blue and cream, softly intermingled; pastel shades.
Coat. To be dense and very soft and silky.
Head and Type. Head broad and round, tiny ears, well placed and well tufted, short broad nose, colour intermingled on face.
Eyes. Deep copper or orange.
Body. Short, cobby and massive, short thick legs.

Scale of Points

Colour	30
Coat and Condition	20
Head and Type	20
Eyes	15
Body	15
Total ..	100

(13a) Any other colours

(8) Brown Tabby – Long-Hairs

Colour and Markings. Rich tawny sable, with delicate black pencillings running down face. The cheeks crossed with two or three distinct swirls. The chest crossed by two unbroken narrow lines, butterfly markings on shoulders. Front of legs striped regularly from toes upwards. The saddle and sides to have deep bands running down them, and the tail to be regularly ringed.
Coat. Long and flowing, tail short and full.
Body. Cobby and massive, short legs.
Head. Round and broad, small well placed and well tufted ears, short broad nose, full round cheeks.
Eyes. Large and round, hazel or copper colour.

Scale of Points

Coat ..	..	..	..	..	50
Body	..	..	..	..	15
Head	..	..	..	..	20
Eyes	..	..	..	..	15
			Total	..	100

(10) Chinchillas

Colour. The undercoat should be pure white, the coat on back, flanks, head, ears and tail being tipped with black, this tipping to be evenly distributed, thus giving the characteristic, sparkling silver appearance; the legs may be very slightly shaded with the tipping, but the chin, ear tufts, stomach slightly shaded with the tipping, but the chin, ear tufts, stomach and chest must be pure white; any tabby markings or brown or cream tinge is a drawback. The tip of the nose should be brick-red, and the visible skin on eyelids and the pads should be black or dark brown.

Head. Broad and round, with breadth between ears and wide at the muzzle; snub nose; small, well tufted ears.

Shape. Cobby body; short, thick legs.

Eyes. Large, round and most expressive, emerald or blue-green in colour.

Coat and Condition. Silky and fine in texture, long and dense, extra long on frill.

Tail. Short and bushy.

Scale of Points

Colour	..	..	..	..	25
Head	..	..	..	..	20
Shape	..	..	..	..	15
Eyes	..	..	..	..	15
Coat and Condition		..	..	..	15
Tail	..	..	..	..	10
			Total	..	100

(6) Smokes

A smoke is a cat of contrasts, the undercolour being as white as possible, with the tips shading to black, the dark points being most defined on the back, head and feet, and the light points on frill, flanks and ear-tufts.

Colour. Body: Black, shading to silver on sides, flanks and mask. Feet: Black, with no markings. Frill and ear-tufts: Silver. Undercolour: As nearly white as possible.

Coat and Condition. Silky texture, long and dense, extra long frill. Shape Head: broad and round, with width between ears, snub nose. Ears: small and tufted. Body: cobby, not coarse but massive, short legs.

Eyes. Orange or copper in colour, large and round in shape, pleasing expression.

Tail. Short and bushy.

Scale of Points

Colour	40
Coat and Condition	20
Shape	20
Eyes	10
Tail	10
Total ..	**100**

N.B. The above is also the standard for Blue Smokes, except that where the word 'black' occurs, 'blue' should be substituted.

(7) Silver Tabby – Long-Hairs

Colour. Ground colour pure pale silver, with decided jet black markings, any brown tinge a drawback.

Head. Broad and round, with breadth between ears and wide at muzzle, short nose, small well tufted ears.

Shape. Cobby body, short thick legs.

Eyes. Gin: green or hazel.

Coat and Condition. Silky in texture, long and dense, extra long on frill.

Tail. Short and bushy.

G

Scale of Points

Colour	.. ..	40
Head	.. ..	20
Shape	.. ..	10
Tail	.. ..	5
Eyes (Green or Hazel)	.. ..	10
Coat and Condition	.. ..	15
	Total ..	**100**

(13a) Any Other Colour

(13b) Colourpoint – Long-Hairs

Coat. Fur long, thick and soft in texture, frill full. Colour to be seal, blue or chocolate-pointed with appropriate body colour as for Siamese (i.e. cream, glacial white or ivory respectively). Points to be dense and body shading, if any, to be the same as the points.

Head. Broad and round with width between ears. Face and nose short. Ears small and tufted and cheeks well developed.

Eyes. SHAPE: large, round and full. COLOUR: clear, bright and decidedly blue, the deeper the better.

Body. Cobby and low on leg.

Tail. Short and full, not tapering (a kink shall be considered a defect).

N.B. Any similarity in TYPE to Siamese to be considered most undesirable and incorrect.

Scale of Points

Coat	.. ..	15
Point and Body Colour	.. ..	10
Head	.. .. ..	25
Shape of Eye	.. ..	10
Colour of Eye	.. ..	10
Body	.. .. ..	10
Tail	.. .. ..	10
Condition	.. .. ..	10
	Total ..	**100**

(13c) Birmans

	Points
Body. Long but cobby. Short strong paws. 4 white paws	20
Head. Wide, round but strongly built with full cheeks	20
Fur. Long with good full ruff, bushy tail, silky texture, slightly curled on belly	25
Eyes. Bright China Blue	5
Tail. Bushy (not short)	10
Colour and Condition. The colouring is the same as Siamese, Seal and Blue but face (mask) tail and paws are dark brown, with the seals and blue/grey with the blues. However, the beige of the coat is slightly golden. The paws are white gloved, this being the characteristic of the Birman cat ..	20
Total ..	100

STANDARDS FOR SHORT-HAIRS

Body and Tail. Well knit and powerful, showing good depth of body. Chest full and broad. Tail thick at base, well set, length in proportion to body.

Legs and Feet. Legs of good substance and in proportion to the body. Feet neat and well rounded.

Head and Neck. Head broad between the ears; cheeks well developed; face and nose short.

Ears. Small, slightly round at tops, not large at base.

Coat. Short, fine and close.

Condition. Hard and muscular, giving a general appearance of activity.

Scale of Points

Body and Tail	10
Legs and Feet	5
Head and Neck	10
Ears	10
Coat	10
Condition	5

G*

The above 50 points apply to all British Short-Hairs and leaves 50 to be apportioned for Colour and Eyes in the individual breeds.

(15) Black Cats – Short-Haired

Points

Colour. Jet black to roots, no rusty tinge, no white hairs anywhere 25

Eyes. Large, round and well opened. COLOUR: deep copper or orange with no trace of green 25

White Cats – Short-Haired

(14) (*Blue-Eyed Whites*)

Points

Colour. White to be pure, untinged with yellow .. 25

Eyes. Very deep sapphire blue 25

(14a) (*Orange-Eyed Whites*)

Colour. White to be pure, untinged with yellow .. 25

Eyes. Golden orange or copper 25

(16) British Blue Cats

Colour. Light to medium blue, very level in colour and no tabby markings or shadings or white anywhere 25

Eyes. Large and full, copper, orange or yellow .. 25

(17) Cream Cats

Colour. Rich cream, level in colour, free from bars; no sign of white anywhere 35

Eyes. Copper or hazel 15

Points

(21) Tortoiseshell Cats

Colour. Black and red (light and dark), equally balanced, and each colour to be as brilliant as possible; no white. Patches to be clear and defined, no blurring and no tabby or brindle markings. Legs, feet, tail and ears to be as well patched as body and head. Red blaze desirable 25

Eyes. Orange, copper or hazel 25

Points

(22) Tortoiseshell-and-White Cats

Colour. Black and red (dark and light), on white,
equally balanced. Colours to be brilliant and
absolutely free from brindling or tabby markings.
The tricolour patchings should cover the top of
head, ears and cheeks, back and tail and part of
flanks. Patches to be clear and defined. White
blaze desirable   50

All structural points to follow those given for Black Cats.
No hard-and-fast rule can be laid down for the patching of
Tortie-and-White Cats and must be left to the individual
judgment. White must never predominate; the reverse is
preferable.

Eyes. Orange, copper or hazel.

Tabby Cats
(20) (*Brown Tabby Cats*)

Points

Markings. Very dense and black, not mixed with the
ground colour and quite distinct from it. Ground
colour rich sable, or brown, uniform throughout,
no white anywhere   50

Eyes. Orange, hazel, deep yellow or green.

(18) (*Silver Tabby Cats*)

Points

Markings. Dense black, not mixed with the ground
colour and quite distinct from it. Ground colour
pure, clear silver, uniform throughout, no white
anywhere   50

Eyes. Round and well opened; colour green or hazel.

(19) (*Red Tabby Cats*)

Markings. Very dense and dark red, not mixed with the
ground colour and quite distinct from it. Ground
colour and markings to be as rich as possible   ..   50

Eyes. Hazel or orange.

(*Mackerel-Striped Tabby Cats*)
(No Breed number, as yet)

Markings. As dense as possible, distinct from ground colour. Rings as narrow and numerous as possible, and running vertically from the spine towards the ground   50

In all Tabby Cats the tails must be neatly ringed, and chest ring or rings most desirable; in fact, almost essential.

(16a) Russian Blue Cats
(Revised 1966)

Colour. Clear Blue, even throughout and in maturity free from tabby markings or shading. Medium blue is preferred.

Coat. Short, thick and very fine, standing up soft and silky like seal skin. Very different from any other breed. Coat is double so that it has a distinct silvery sheen. The texture and appearance of the coat is the truest criterion of the Russian Blue.

Body and Tail. Body long and graceful in outline and carriage. Medium strong bone. Tail fairly long and tapering.

Legs and Feet. Legs long, feet small and oval.

Head. Short wedge, with flat skull: forehead and nose straight, forming an angle. Prominent whisker pads.

Eyes. Vivid green, set rather wide apart, almond in shape.

Ears. Large and pointed, wide at base and set vertically to the head. Skin of ears thin and transparent, with very little inside furnishing.

Faults. White or tabby markings: Cobby or heavy build: Square head: Yellow in eyes. Siamese type is undesirable.

Scale of Points

Colour	20
Coat and condition	25
Body, build and tail	25
Eyes	15
Head and ears	15
Total ..	100

(25) Manx Cats

Taillessness, height of hindquarters, shortness of back and depth of flank are essentials in a Manx Cat, as only with them is combined the true rabbity or hopping gait. The coat is what is termed 'double', namely, soft and open like that of a rabbit, with a soft, thick under-coat. That is another essential and great attention should be paid to roundness of rump – as round as an orange being the ideal.

Scale of Points

Taillessness	15
Height of Hindquarters	15
Shortness of Back	15
Roundness of Rump	10
Depth of Flank	10
Double Coat	10
Head and Ears	10
Colour and Markings	5
Eyes	5
Condition	5
Total ..	100

Remarks

Taillessness must be absolute in a show specimen. There should be a decided hollow at the end of the backbone, where in the ordinary cat the tail would begin. The hindquarters in a Manx cannot be too high, and the back cannot be too short, where there must be a great depth of flank. The head is round and large, but it is not a snubby or Persian type. The nose is longish, but the cheeks being very prominent do away with snipyness, which is a bad fault. The ears are rather wide at base, tapering slightly off to a point. Eye colour is of very secondary consideration, and must only be taken into account when all other points are equal. When that is so, it follows the ideal for the British Cats, namely, blue for whites and amber or orange for blacks, oranges, tortoiseshells, etc. All colours of Manx are recognised, and here, again, as in eye-colour, marking and colour must only be taken into account when all other points are equal. Finally, gait, arising from the combination referred to in the opening sentence, is of primary importance.

(28) Blue-Cream Short-Hairs

Type. Body shape, head and eyes, as for British Blue Cats.
Eyes. copper, orange or yellow (not green).
Coat. Colours to be softly mingled, not patched, short and fine in texture.

Scale of Points

Type, as for British Cats	40
Colour, mingling	35
Eyes	20
Condition	5
Total ..	100

(23) Abyssinians

Colour and Type. Ruddy brown, ticked with black or dark brown, double or treble ticking – i.e., two or three bands of colour on each hair preferably to single ticking; no bars or other markings except that a dark spine line will not militate against an otherwise good specimen. Inside of forelegs and belly should be of a tint to harmonise well with the main colour, the preference being given to orange-brown.

Absence of Markings. i.e., bars on head, tail, face and chest – is a very important property in this breed. These places are just where, if a cat or other feline animal shows markings at all, they will hold their ground to the last with remarkable pertinacity. The less markings visible the better; at the same time the judge must not attach such undue importance to this property that he fails to give due importance to others. For instance, it does not follow that an absolutely unmarked cat, but of 'cobby' build, failing in ticking and colour is, on account of absence of marking, better than a cat of slender build, well ticked, and of nice colour, but handicapped by a certain amount of 'barring' on legs and tail.

Head and Ears. Head long and pointed, ears sharp, comparatively large and broad at base.

Eyes. Large, bright and expressive. Green, yellow or hazel in colour.

Tail. Fairly long and tapering.

Feet. Small, pads black: this colour also extending up the back of the hind legs.

Coat. Short, fine and close.

Size. Never large or coarse.

Scale of Points

Colour:

Body Colour	30	
Ticking	20	
	—	
		50

Type:

Head and ears	15	
Eyes	5	
Body shape, tail, feet, coat and carriage	20	
General condition ..	10	
	—	
		50

Total ..	100	

N.B. Although imperfect cats may be awarded prizes according to the merit of the entry, no Abyssinians should be awarded a champion certificate that has distinct bars and rings on legs and tail, white chin to be considered undesirable, other white markings not permissible.

(23a) Red Abyssinians

The Red Abyssinian is the same in every respect as the Standard Abyssinian, except for colour which is as follows:

The body colour is rich copper red, doubly, or preferably trebly, ticked with darker colours. Lack of distinct contrast in the ticking is a fault. The richer the body colour the better. A pale coat is a bad fault.

The belly and inside of legs should be deep apricot to harmonize. The tail tip is dark brown and this may extend along the tail as a line. A spine line of deeper colour is permissible. The nose leather is pink. Pads are pink, set in brown fur which extends up the back of the legs. Eye colour is the same as for Standard Abyssinians.

N.B. As with Standard Abyssinians, a white chin is to be considered undesirable and other white markings are not permissible.

(24) Siamese (Seal-Pointed)

Shape (Body and Tail). Medium in size, body long and svelte, legs proportionately slim, hind legs slightly higher than the front ones, feet small and oval, tail long and tapering (either straight or slightly kinked at the extremity).

The body, legs, feet, head and tail all in proportion, giving the whole a well-balanced appearance.

Head and Ears. Head long and well proportioned, with width between the eyes, narrowing in perfectly straight lines to a fine muzzle, giving the impression of a marten face. Ears rather large and pricked, wide at the base.

Eyes. Clear, brilliant deep blue. Shape oriental and slanting towards the nose. No tendency to squint.

Body Colour. Cream, shading gradually into pale warm fawn on the back. Kittens paler in colour.

Points. Mask, ears, legs, feet and tail dense and clearly defined seal brown. Mask complete and (except in kittens) connected by tracing with the ears.

Coat. Very short and fine in texture, glossy and close-lying.

Notes and Definitions

Definition of Squint. When the eyes are so placed that they appear to look permanently at the nose.

N.B. The Siamese Cat should be a beautifully balanced animal with head, ears and neck carried on a long svelte body, supported on fine legs and feet with a tail in proportion. The head and profile should be wedge-shaped, neither round nor pointed. The mask complete connected by tracings with the ears (except in kittens), the eyes a deep blue, green tinge to be considered a fault. Expression alert and intelligent.

White toes or toe to automatically disqualify an exhibit. It is important to note that the Standard with regard to Type and Shape is the same for all Siamese Cats.

Value of Points

Type and Shape

Head	..	..	..	15
Ears	..	..	..	5
Eyes	..	..	..	5
				—
				25
Body	..	..	..	15
Legs and Paws	..	..		5
Tail	..	..	..	5
				—
				25
				—
		Total	..	50

Colour

Eyes	..	..	..	15
Points	..	..	..	10
Body Colour	..	..		10
				—
				35
Texture of coat	..	..		10
Condition	..	..		5
				—
				15
		Total	..	50

(24a) Siamese (Blue-Pointed)

The Standard is the same as for Seal-Pointed with the following exceptions:

Colour. Points blue, the ears, mask, legs, paws and tail to be the same colour. The ears should not be darker than the other points.

Eyes. Clear, bright, vivid blue.

Body. Body colour, glacial white, shading gradually into blue on the back, the same cold tone as the points but of a lighter shade.

Texture of Coat. The same as for Seal-Pointed.

(24b) Siamese (Chocolate-Pointed)

The Standard is the same as for Seal-Pointed with the following exceptions :

Colour. Points milk chocolate, the ears, mask, legs, paws and tail to be the same colour, the ears should not be darker than the other points.

Eyes. Clear, bright, vivid blue.

Body. Ivory colour all over. Shading, if at all, to be the colour of points.

Texture of Coat. The same as for Seal-Pointed.

(24c) Siamese (Lilac-Pointed)

The Standard is the same as for Seal-Pointed with the following exceptions :

Eyes. Same description as for Blue-Points.

Points. Frosty grey of pinkish tone.

Nose Leather and Pads. Faded lilac.

Body Colour. Frosty white shading, if any, to tone with points.

Texture of Coat. As for all Siamese.

Number of points to be awarded for any feature to be the same as for all Siamese.

(26) Any Other Variety
(27) Burmese Cats

Standard of Points for an experimental period of two years.

Points

Body Colour. In full maturity the body should be a solid colour of rich dark seal brown shading to slightly lighter on chest and belly. No white or tabby markings. Ears, mask and points only slightly darker than back coat colour. Awards should be withheld from mature cats showing decided contrast between coat colour and points ..   25
In kittens and young cats all colours may be slightly lighter in colour with greater contrast allowed between coat colour, mask and points. Kittens still lighter generally.

Body, Shape and Tail. The body should be medium in

size, dainty, long and svelte. Neck long and slender, legs proportionately slim, hind legs slightly higher than front, feet small and oval in shape. Tail long and tapering to a point. A slight kink at the extreme tip only is permissible .. 25

Points

Head and Ears. Head short wedge with slight rounding on top. Ears pricked, relatively large and wide at base 15

Eyes. Yellow almond in shape and slanting towards the nose in true Oriental fashion. Blue eyes and squints inadmissible 15

Coat. Glossy, short, fine in texture and lying close to the body 10

Condition. Excellent physical condition, not fat, inclined to muscle. 10

Total .. 100

(27a) Blue Burmese

Points

Body Colour. The body colour of the adult should be predominantly bluish grey, darker on back, the overall effect being a warm colour, with a silver sheen to the coat. The tail the same colour as the back, no white or tabby markings. Ears, mask and feet shading to silver grey. Kittens lighter in colour 25

Body Shape and Tail. The body should be medium in size, dainty, long and svelte. Neck long and slender, legs proportionately slim, hind legs slightly higher than front, feet small and oval in shape. Tail long and tapering to a point. A slight kink at extreme tip only is permissible 25

Head and Ears. Head, short wedge with slight rounding on top. Ears pricked, relatively large and wide at base 15

Eyes. Yellowish green. Almond in shape and slanting
  towards the nose in true Oriental fashion. Blue
  eyes and squints inadmissible   15
Coat. Fine, glossy, short and lying close to the body   10
Condition. Excellent physical condition, not fat,
  inclined to muscle   10
                                                          ————
                                    Total   ..   100

N.B. It is recommended that only cats of true Burmese parentage
  be eligible for Championship status.

(29) Chestnut Brown Foreign

Chestnut Brown Cats are of foreign type. They are fine in bone,
  lithe and sinuous and of graceful proportions. The coat is a
  rich brown, even and sound, whiskers and nose to be of the
  same colour as the coat. The pads of the feet are a pinkish
  shade. The eyes are green.
Coat. Any shade of rich chestnut brown, short and glossy, even
  and sound throughout.
Head and Ears. Head long and well proportioned, narrowing
  to a fine muzzle, ears large and pricked, wide at the base
  with good width between.
Body, Legs and Tail. Body long, lithe and well muscled, graceful
  in outline. Legs slim and dainty, hind legs slightly higher
  than front legs. Paws oval and neat. Long whip tail, no kink.
Eyes. Slanting and oriental in shape, decidedly green in colour.

Scale of Points

Coat ..	..	..	.. ..	..	30
Head	..	..	..	..	15
Body	..	..	..	..	15
Legs	..	..	..	..	15
Tail ..	..	..	..	..	5
Eyes	..	..	..	..	10
Condition	..	..	..	..	10
					————
		Total	..		100

Faults. Tabby or other markings, dark points, whitespots or hairs, cobby shape, round head, short thick or kinked tail.

N.B. Kittens frequently show tabby 'ghost' markings when changing coat. This should not be held against an otherwise good kitten exhibit.

(30) Spotted Cats

In judging Spotted Cats, good and clear spotting is the first essential. The Spots can be round, oblong or rosette-shaped. Any of these markings may be of equal merit, but the spots, however shaped or placed shall be distinct and not running into each other. They may be of any colour as suitable to the ground colouration. Colour of eyes to conform to coat colour.

Faults. Stripes and bars (except on face and head): brindling. Judging by points a value of 50 should be allotted to spotting, after which the ordinary British Short-Haired Cat properties may be valued at the remaining 50 points.

(31) Bi-coloured

Points

Colour. Black and white, Blue and white, Orange and white, Cream and white. No tabby shadings in the self-coloured portion   20

Marking. The self-colour, i.e., Black, Blue, Cream or Orange to start immediately behind the shoulders, round the barrel of body, and to include tail and hind legs, leaving the hind feet wide. Ears and mask of face also self-coloured. White shoulders, neck and forelegs and feet, chin, lips and blaze up face and over top of head, joining or running into the white at back of skull, thus dividing the mask exactly in half. The markings to follow those of a Dutch-marked Rabbit as closely as possible   25

Eyes. Copper, orange or amber   5

The remaining 50 points to be apportioned according to the Standard laid down for all British Short-Haired Cats.

(32) Tabby Point Siamese

Type. As for Siamese.

Head. Wide at the top and tapering to a pointed nose. A strong chin.

Ears. Large and pricked, wide at base.

Nose. Rather long and clearly defined.

Eyes. Oriental in shape, slanting towards the nose.

Neck. Rather long and graceful, but strong.

Body. Long and svelte.

Legs. Long and slim.

Feet. Small and oval in shape.

Tail. Long and tapering.

Description. A cat of medium size, virile and muscular but dainty in appearance.

Colour.

General Body Colour. Pale and free from markings.

Ears. Solid, no stripes. Thumb mark.

Nose Black, brown or pink.

Mask. Clearly defined stripes especially round the eyes and nose. Distinct markings on cheeks, darkly spotted whisker pads.

Eyes. Brilliant clear blue. The lids rimmed with black.

Legs. Varied sized broken stripes, solid markings on back of legs.

Feet. No markings.

Tail. Varied sized clearly defined rings ending in a solid tip.

Coat. Close lying and firm.

Value of Points

Type and Shape

Head	..	..	..	15
Ears	..	..	..	5
Eyes	..	..	..	5
Body	..	..	..	15
Legs and Feet	..	..		5
Tail	..	..	..	5
				50

Colour

Eyes	..	..	..	15
Body Colour		..	..	10
Points	..	..	..	10
Texture of Coat	..		..	10
Condition			..	5
				——
				50

Total   ..   100

Red Point and Tortie Siamese

Points

Type and Shape. As for Sealpoint Siamese   50
Head. Wide at the top and tapering to a pointed
nose. A strong chin   15
Ears. Large, wide at the base, but pricked   5
Nose. Rather long and clearly defined   ..   ..
Eyes. Oriental in shape, slanting towards the nose.
No squint   5
Neck. Long and graceful but strong   ..   ..   ..
Body. Long and svelte   15
Legs. Long and slim, hind legs slightly higher than
front; *Feet*. Small and oval in shape   5
Tail. Long and tapering, straight or slightly kinked
at the extremity   5
Description. A cat of medium size, virile and muscular
but dainty in appearance.

(32a) Red Points

Points

Colour.   50
Body. White, shading (if any) to apricot on the back.
Kittens paler   10
Nose. Pink   ..   ..
Ears. Bright reddish-gold. *Mask*. Bright reddish-gold   10
Legs and feet. Bright reddish-gold or apricot   ..
Tail. Bright reddish-gold   ..   ..
Eyes. Bright vivid blue   15
Coat. Short, fine silky hair, glossy and close-lying   ..   10

Condition 5

Modification. Barring or striping on mask, legs or tail is not to be deemed a fault.

(32b) Tortie Point

Tortie Points. Restricted to the points, as in all Siamese, basic colour as in Sealpoint Siamese

Colour 50

Body. Cream or fawn, shading (if any) to match basic colour of points 10

Points

Nose. As Sealpoint Siamese .. .. ..

Ears. Seal sprinkled with red (which must be clearly visible), or red sprinkled with Seal .. ..

Mask. Seal defined as in Sealpoint Siamese, with tracings up to the ears, traces of red permissible, distribution of cream and seal to be in equal proportions, evenness of patching not essential .. ..

Legs and feet. Basic colour in accordance with mask, marbled with red or ivory or both 10

Tail. Basic colour according to mask, brindled cream, solid and of basic colour permissible .. ..

Eyes. Brilliant deep blue 15

Coat. Short, fine silky hair, glossy and close-lying .. 10

Condition 5

(32c) Any Other Dilution Siamese

These new variations, though recognized as Siamese, are not yet eligible for championships.

(33) Cornish Rex

Coat. Dense, very short and fine, forming waves over the entire body with the exception of the head, legs and paws where the coat should resemble dense short plush. Whiskers and eyebrows to be crinkled. All recognised coat colours and coat patterns acceptable.

Head. Medium to long, well proportioned and narrowing to a strong chin. The skull to be flat. In profile a straight line is to be seen from the centre of forehead to nose end.

Eyes. Almond shape, medium size, colour in keeping with coat colour and coat pattern.

Ears. Large, set rather high on head, wide at base, tapering to rounded tops, well covered with fine fur.

Body, Neck and Legs. Body long and slender, hard and muscular, medium in size, legs long and fine giving an overall appearance of being high on the legs. Paws small and oval. Neck slender.

Tail. Long, fine and whiplike.

Scale of Points

Coat ..	..	..	..	..	50
Head	..	..	..	..	5
Eyes	..	..	..	..	5
Ears ..	..	..	..	..	10
Body, neck and legs			..	..	25
Tail ..	..	..	..	..	5
			Total	..	100

Faults. British Type head, cobby body, small ears, lack of firm muscles. Short tail, white mismarkings.

N.B. If all other points are equal preference should be given to the cat whose coat does not show white hairs or markings other than those under coat.

(33a) Devon Rex

Coat. Dense, very short and fine, forming waves over the entire body with the exception of the head, legs and paws where the coat should resemble dense short plush. Whiskers and eyebrows to be crinkled. All recognised coat colours and coat patterns acceptable.

Head. Face to be full cheeked with considerable width between the eyes. Medium wedge with whisker break. Short muzzle. Nose with a definite stop in profile. Forehead to slope back to a flat skull.

Eyes. Rather large. Almond shaped with outer corners pointing to outer edges of ears. Colour in keeping with coat colour and coat pattern or chartreuse green or yellow.

Ears. Large, set rather low, great width at base gradually tapering to rounded tops. Well covered. Kittens may have ear muffs.

Body, Neck and Legs. Body long and slender, hard and muscular, medium in size. Legs long and fine, giving an overall appearance of being high on the legs. Paws small and oval. Neck slender.

Tail. Long, fine and whiplike.

Scale of Points

Coat ..	..	..	..	..	45
Head	..	..	..	..	10
Eyes	..	..	..	..	5
Ears ..	..	..	..	..	10
Body, neck and legs			..	..	25
Tail	..	..	..	..	5
			Total	..	100

Faults. British type head, cobby body, small ears. Lack of firm muscles. Short tail. White mismarkings. Bareness to be considered a fault, but cats should not be penalised too heavily for this for the time being.

N.B. If all other points are equal preference should be given to the cat whose coat does not show white hairs or markings other than those under coat.